MW01440579

Exploring America's National Parks

A Guide to the Wild Splendor and
Secret Marvels of Our Most
Treasured Natural Landscapes

W. R. Hoover

© **Copyright RLL Publishing 2024 - All rights reserved.**
The content within this book may not be reproduced, duplicated or transmitted without direct written permission from the author or the publisher.
Under no circumstances will any blame or legal responsibility be held against the publisher, or author, for any damages, reparation, or monetary loss due to the information contained within this book. Either directly or indirectly. You are responsible for your own choices, actions, and results.

Legal Notice:
This book is copyright protected. This book is only for personal use. You cannot amend, distribute, sell, use, quote or paraphrase any part, of the content within this book, without the consent of the author or publisher.

Disclaimer Notice:
Please note the information contained within this document is for educational and entertainment purposes only. All effort has been expended to present accurate, up-to-date, and reliable, complete information. No warranties of any kind are declared or implied. Readers acknowledge that the author is not engaging in the rendering of legal, financial, medical or professional advice. The content within this book has been derived from various sources. Please consult a licensed professional before attempting any techniques outlined in this book. By reading this document, the reader agrees that under no circumstances is the author responsible for any losses, direct or indirect, which are incurred as a result of the use of the information contained within this document, including, but not limited to, — errors, omissions, or inaccuracies.

Table of Contents

Introduction *1*

Chapter 1: The Jewels of the West *3*

    1.1 Yosemite's Secret Trails: Beyond the Valley 4

    1.2 Night Skies of Joshua Tree: Stargazing and Photography 5

    1.3 The Geothermal Wonders of Yellowstone Off the Beaten Path 7

    1.4 Hiking the Tetons: Safety and Solitude 10

    1.5 Zion's Lesser-Known Canyons: A Guide for the Adventurous 12

    1.6 Glacier National Park: Accessible Trails for All Abilities 14

Chapter 2: The Coastal and Tropical Treasures *17*

    2.1 Kayaking in Everglades National Park: A Water Adventure 17

    2.2 Olympic National Park: From Mountains to Tide Pools 19

    2.3 Hawaii Volcanoes National Park: Lava Viewing Tips and Safety... 23

    2.4 Channel Islands: Snorkeling and Marine Life Conservation 25

    2.5 Acadia National Park: Cycling the Carriage Roads 26

    2.6 Virgin Islands National Park: Sustainable Tourism and Coral Reefs 29

Chapter 3: The Heartlands and the Mountains *31*

    3.1 The Smoky Mountains: Seasonal Wildflowers and Wildlife 31

    3.2 Rocky Mountain National Park: High Altitude Hiking Tips 34

    3.3 Badlands National Park: Otherworldly Geology and Stargazing... 37

    3.4 The Caves of Wind Cave National Park: Underground Exploration 39

    3.5 The Bison of Theodore Roosevelt National Park: Viewing with Respect 41

    3.6 Cuyahoga Valley National Park: A Historical Journey 43

Chapter 4: The Desert Landscapes *46*

    4.1 Death Valley's Superblooms: Nature's Resilience 46

4.2 Arches National Park: Photography Without Crowds 49

4.3 Petrified Forest National Park: A Journey Through Time 51

4.4 Big Bend National Park: Stargazing and Solitude 54

4.5 Saguaro National Park: The Giants of the Desert 55

4.6 White Sands National Park: Sledding on Gypsum Dunes 58

Chapter 5: Trip Planning and Logistics 65

5.1 Navigating Peak Seasons: Best Times to Visit 65

5.2 Budget-Friendly National Park Vacations: Tips and Tricks 67

5.3 Packing for the Parks: Essentials for Every Climate 69

5.4 Finding the Perfect Place to Stay: Lodging Inside and Near the Parks 71

5.5 Accessibility in the Parks: Ensuring an Inclusive Experience 74

5.6 The Digital Nomad's Guide to National Parks: Connectivity Spots 76

Chapter 6: Safety, Conservation, and Etiquette 79

6.1 Wildlife Encounters: Safety and Respect 79

6.2 Leave No Trace: Principles for Park Visitors 81

6.3 Fire Safety in National Parks: A Critical Guide 83

6.4 Conserving Water in Desert Parks: Do's and Don'ts 85

6.5 Cultural Heritage Sites: Visiting with Respect 87

6.6 Reporting Issues: How Visitors Can Help 89

Chapter 7: Activities and Experiences 91

7.1 Best National Park Hikes for Every Fitness Level 92

7.2 Capturing the Moment: Photography Tips for Amateurs 95

7.3 The Park Ranger Experience: Programs and Tours 97

7.4 Nighttime in the Parks: From Campfires to Star Parties 99

7.5 The Solitude of Winter: Snowshoeing and Cross-Country Skiing 101

7.6 Water Activities: From Rafting to Fishing 104

Chapter 8: Beyond the Beaten Path *108*

    8.1 North Cascades National Park: America's Best-Kept Secret 108

    8.2 The Quiet Side of Grand Canyon: North Rim Adventures 110

    8.3 Exploring the Lesser-Known Islands of Channel Islands National Park 112

    8.4 Biking Through Big South Fork National River and Recreation Area 114

    8.5 Bird Watching in Congaree National Park: A Hidden Gem 115

    8.6 Backpacking in Isle Royale National Park: Tips for a Remote Adventure 117

Conclusion *120*

List of America's National Parks *122*

References *124*

Introduction

Have you ever stood where the earth meets the sky, where each breath unveils a view so vast it stretches the very seams of your imagination? This is the essence of America's national parks—a tapestry of landscapes so vivid and diverse that each visit feels like the first. Whether it is the thunderous applause of Old Faithful under the big Wyoming sky or the serene silence of the giant redwoods in California, these parks are a testament to nature's splendor.

Embark on a thrilling adventure through these majestic parks, guided by firsthand experiences. My journey into the heart of America's natural wonders began with a breathtaking sunrise at Acadia National Park, where the Atlantic Ocean meets rugged cliffs. That morning, as the sky transformed into a canvas of colors, my love for these parks was born. Since then, I have ventured onto lesser-known trails, camped under the starry skies, and learned to listen to the whispers of the wilderness. These experiences have revealed the beauty of these lands and instilled in me the importance of preserving them for future generations, sparking a sense of adventure and discovery in me that I hope to share with you.

This guidebook is your exclusive pass to uncovering the secrets of these natural paradises. It is meticulously designed not just to lead you but to ignite your curiosity and enrich your knowledge. You will delve into comprehensive narratives of each park, from the renowned to the hidden, accompanied by practical travel advice and captivating visuals. This is not your typical travel guide; it is a profound exploration of the less-traveled paths, the concealed corners, and the untold tales behind the landscapes.

These parks are not merely picturesque landscapes but vital for conservation, serving as sanctuaries for countless species and natural ecosystems. Through my lens, you will witness their magnificence and understand their pivotal role in our natural heritage. They are not just a part of our shared duty, but a responsibility we all bear in protecting them for future generations, fostering a profound sense of connection and responsibility in each of us.

Designed to cater to a diverse range of travelers, this guidebook is divided into sections highlighting each park's unique features, hidden treasures, and essential advice for accommodation and exploration. Whether planning a family getaway, a solo expedition, or a tranquil retreat into nature's serenity, this guide will be your reliable compass and creative inspiration.

As we turn these pages together, consider this book more than a planning tool—it is a call to adventure. Embrace these destinations with respect and curiosity while you join in the efforts to keep them pristine and thriving.

Reflecting on my journey through the vast landscapes of the Grand Canyon, I invite you to begin your exploration. Let every national park visit challenge and change you; let it be a journey of discovery, respect, and awe. Welcome to a celebration of America's greatest natural treasures—allow us to begin this unforgettable adventure together.

Chapter 1: The Jewels of the West

Figure 1 Majestic granite cliffs of Yosemite National Park

As dawn creeps softly over the rugged peaks of the Sierra Nevada, the first rays of sunlight glaze the granite cliffs of Yosemite, casting a golden hue that enchants the eye. This iconic landscape, famed for its breathtaking vistas and towering waterfalls, is more than just a feast for the senses; it is a gateway to lesser-known paths where silence speaks the language of our ancient earth. Yosemite National Park, a cornerstone of America's natural heritage, offers a deeper communion with nature through its hidden trails and secluded spots. Here, you can tread lightly on the less traveled paths, where each step unveils a new perspective, and each breath deepens your connection with the wild.

1.1 Yosemite's Secret Trails: Beyond the Valley

Hidden Hikes: Discover trails less traveled for serene views and unique park perspectives.

While the bustling valley floor of Yosemite draws millions of visitors, the park's lesser-known trails offer serene escapes and highlight its grandeur from unique vantage points. Trails like the Ostrander Lake path lead you through peaceful meadows and dense pine forests, culminating at a pristine glacial lake that mirrors the sky. Another hidden gem, the Snow Creek Trail, presents a challenging trek away from the crowds, rewarding the persistent hiker with unparalleled views of Half Dome and the surrounding peaks. These trails are not just pathways through the landscape; they are journeys into the heart of Yosemite's wilderness, where the quiet majesty of nature speaks to those who listen.

Wildlife Watching Opportunities: Tips for spotting Yosemite's diverse wildlife in quieter areas.

Yosemite is a sanctuary for an array of wildlife, from majestic deer to elusive bobcats, and the secret trails offer some of the best opportunities to encounter these creatures in their natural habitats. Early morning or dusk are prime times for wildlife spotting, as animals are most active during these cooler parts of the day. Hiking quietly without the noise of crowds increases your chances of observing these animals. Keep your eyes peeled for signs of wildlife, such as tracks, scat, or nibbled vegetation. Binoculars are a valuable tool, allowing you to watch from a distance without disturbing the animals' natural behaviors.

Seasonal Considerations: The best times to visit these secret trails to avoid crowds and experience natural beauty.

The secret trails of Yosemite are most tranquil during the shoulder seasons—late spring and early fall—when the bulk of tourists have not yet arrived or have just departed. The weather is mild during these times, and the changing seasons paint the landscape spectacularly. Spring brings blooming wildflowers and gushing waterfalls, a perfect backdrop for your hikes. In the fall, the crisp air is filled with pine aroma, and the leaves become a tapestry of fiery hues. Visiting during these seasons ensures a more isolated experience and displays Yosemite's dynamic ecosystems in their most dramatic transformations.

Conservation Efforts: How respectful exploration of lesser-known areas can contribute to the park's preservation.

Exploring Yosemite's lesser-known trails can also play a part in the park's conservation efforts. By distributing visitor traffic more evenly across the park, we reduce the strain on the most popular areas, helping to preserve the natural terrain and minimize erosion. Practicing Leave No Trace principles is crucial as you enjoy the hidden trails. This means staying on designated paths, packing out all trash, and respecting wildlife habitats. These actions ensure that the park's secluded areas remain pristine and their ecosystems continue to thrive, safeguarding Yosemite's natural heritage for future generations.

Traveling these secret paths offers more than just a physical journey; it is an exploration of the soul amidst the quiet grandeur of nature. As you wander through Yosemite's hidden landscapes, you engage with the park more intimately, discovering its physical beauty and vital role in our ecological and cultural history.

1.2 Night Skies of Joshua Tree: Stargazing and Photography

Joshua Tree National Park, a convergence of the Mojave and Colorado deserts, offers more than surreal landscapes and unique flora. It presents a celestial theater for some of the clearest night sky views in the Western United States. The park's high elevation, dry climate, and remote location shield it from the light pollution of major cities, making it an ideal spot for stargazing and astrophotography. Among the prime locations for night sky enthusiasts, the areas around Hidden Valley and Barker Dam provide expansive horizons unobstructed by natural formations, where the Milky Way often appears so close you could almost touch it. Another exceptional spot is Arch Rock, where the natural arch frames the cosmos, offering a stunning composition for photographers.

Figure 2 Milky Way galaxy arching over Joshua Tree National Park

Capturing the Milky Way and the intricate dance of celestial bodies requires patience and technique. For those eager to photograph this natural wonder, a digital SLR camera with manual mode is essential, allowing control over exposure settings critical for night photography. A wide-angle lens with a large aperture, such as f/2.8, helps capture the sky's vastness and the subtleties of light. Setting up a tripod stabilizes your camera for long exposures, typically 15 to 30 seconds, necessary to allow enough light to enter the lens without blurring the stars into streaks.

A remote shutter release or the camera's built-in timer further reduces camera shake. Experimenting with different ISO settings, from 1600 upwards, can help find the right balance between exposure and image noise, which can be particularly challenging in night photography.

The allure of Joshua Tree's night skies also emphasizes preserving these dark sky areas. Light pollution not only detracts from the beauty of the night sky but also disrupts the natural rhythms of many desert species that rely on the cover of darkness for survival. Joshua Tree is recognized as a Dark Sky Park as designated by the International Dark-Sky Association. It underscores the park's commitment to protecting its nocturnal environment through responsible lighting policies and public education on the importance of dark skies. Visitors to the park play a crucial role in these conservation efforts by using minimal lighting during their nighttime explorations and participating in ranger-led programs highlighting the importance of dark sky preservation.

Safety is a paramount concern when venturing into the park after dark. The desert's rugged terrain can be treacherous at night, with risks ranging from tripping over unseen rocks to encountering nocturnal wildlife. It is advisable to prepare meticulously for nighttime adventures; this includes familiarizing oneself with the terrain during daylight hours, carrying a map and compass (GPS devices can fail), and packing adequate water and layers to adapt to the sharp drop in temperature after sunset. A flashlight with a red bulb or filter minimizes light pollution while preserving night vision. Always let someone know your plans and expected return time, as cell service in the park can be unreliable. These precautions ensure that your nocturnal experience in Joshua Tree is memorable and safe.

1.3 The Geothermal Wonders of Yellowstone Off the Beaten Path

Yellowstone National Park, a marvel of geothermal activity, is home to more than half the world's geysers and an array of hot springs, mudpots, and fumaroles. While the famous Old Faithful geyser attracts most of the park's visitors, numerous lesser-known geothermal features are scattered throughout this vast landscape, offering a more secluded and equally spectacular experience. In the park's quieter corners, you can find hidden springs and geysers that allow for reflection and appreciation of nature's incredible power without the crowds. One such place is the Lone Star Geyser. A cone geyser located five miles away from the bustling Old Faithful area. It erupts approximately every three hours and provides a serene viewing experience for those who journey there. Another less frequented area is the Porcelain Basin, part of Norris Geyser Basin, which offers a surreal landscape of brightly colored and highly acidic geothermal features, where steam seems to rise from the earth at every turn.

Figure 3 Lone Star Geyser erupting in Yellowstone National Park

Understanding the fragile ecosystem of geothermal areas is crucial for anyone visiting Yellowstone. These features operate within a delicate balance, where even minor changes in human activity can have significant impacts. The heat-loving microorganisms that create the vivid colors around hot springs are susceptible to disturbances. When visitors stray from designated boardwalks and trails, they risk injury and threaten these microbial communities. The park's extensive network of boardwalks is designed to protect visitors and the natural features they have come to see. By staying on marked paths and observing all safety signs, visitors help preserve the integrity of these geothermal wonders for future generations.

When exploring these thermal areas, one can choose between guided tours and solo exploration. Guided tours can offer in-depth knowledge and a structured path through complex geothermal basins, led by experts who know the safest and most informative routes. These tours often provide insights into the geology and biology of the hot springs and geysers and the history and cultural aspects of the areas. For those who prefer a solitary experience, careful preparation is essential. Obtaining up-to-date information from visitor centers, studying park maps, and preparing for sudden weather changes are imperative. Whether choosing a guided tour or exploring independently, the primary consideration should always be safety and environmental respect.

The geology behind Yellowstone's thermal features is as fascinating as it is complex. The park sits atop a volcanic hotspot, a plume of molten rock deep within the Earth's mantle that heats groundwater trapped beneath the surface. When this water becomes superheated, it expands, seeking escape through cracks in the earth, resulting in the explosive eruptions of geysers or the bubbling waters of hot springs. The varying temperatures and chemical compositions of these features create a dynamic, constantly changing geothermal landscape. Each geyser, hot spring, mudpot, and fumarole is a unique window into the powerful geothermal forces that continue to shape Yellowstone. Understanding this dynamic geology adds a profound depth to the experience of visiting these thermal wonders, transforming a simple act of observation into an appreciation of the vibrant forces that drive our planet.

1.4 Hiking the Tetons: Safety and Solitude

Figure 4 Grand Tetons mountain range

The Grand Tetons, with their jagged peaks rising dramatically against Wyoming's expansive skies, offer some of the most unforgettable hiking experiences in the United States. The allure of these mountains is not just in their breathtaking beauty but also in the profound sense of solitude they offer. Here, one can truly immerse in nature's embrace, away from the clamor of daily life. However, the rugged terrain of the Tetons demands respect and preparation; the wilderness is as unforgiving as it is beautiful. Proper planning and gear are paramount for a safe and enjoyable adventure in these mountains. Before setting foot on the trail, ensure you are equipped with sturdy hiking boots that offer good ankle support—crucial for navigating rocky paths. A topographical map and a reliable compass (or GPS device) are essential, not just as tools for navigation but as lifelines in an environment where paths are not always clearly marked. Weather in the Tetons can change swiftly, and what starts as a sunny morning might soon turn into a cold, foggy afternoon. Hence, dressing in layers and carrying a waterproof jacket are wise precautions. Finally, as you pack your backpack, remember that every ounce counts; prioritize lightweight, high-energy food, water, and a first aid kit.

Selecting the right trail in the Tetons can significantly enhance your experience, particularly if you seek solitude. While popular paths like the Jenny Lake Loop offer stunning views, they also attract more foot traffic. For those looking to escape into tranquility, trails such as the Teton Crest Trail offer more isolated stretches where the sounds of nature dominate. Another less trodden path is the hike to Lake Solitude—a fittingly named destination that promises serene landscapes and a challenging journey. This trek, involving steep climbs and rocky terrains, rewards hikers with sweeping views of the Teton range and a peaceful lakeside resting spot. When choosing your trail, consider your fitness level and comfort with isolation, as some quieter paths require more self-reliance and hiking expertise.

Encounters with wildlife are a profound reminder of the Tetons' wild nature. The park is home to creatures ranging from the elusive mountain lion to the majestic moose. While these encounters can be thrilling, they require caution and respect for the animals' space. Maintain a safe distance, especially from larger animals like bears and moose, which can be unpredictable and dangerous if provoked. If you plan to hike during dawn or dusk—when wildlife is most active—it is wise to carry bear spray as a precaution. Moreover, making noise by talking or clapping can alert animals to your presence, reducing the chances of a surprise encounter. Remember, these creatures are not mere spectacles but wild and integral to the Tetons' ecosystem. Observing them with respect ensures your safety and their well-being.

Adhering to Leave No Trace principles is not just about maintaining the aesthetic beauty of the Tetons; it is about preserving its ecological integrity. The principle of packing out what you pack in is fundamental—everything from wrappers to fruit peels must leave the park with you. Stick to established trails to prevent soil erosion and protect undergrowth. If you need to relieve yourself, do so two hundred feet away from any water source, trail, or campsite, and bury human waste in a small hole 6-8 inches deep. These practices may seem minor, but collectively, they have a significant impact on maintaining the health and beauty of the Tetons for future generations to explore and enjoy. As you traverse these ancient mountains, each step taken with care and consideration reinforces your role as a visitor and steward of one of Earth's most awe-inspiring landscapes.

1.5 Zion's Lesser-Known Canyons: A Guide for the Adventurous

Canyoneering in Zion National Park offers more than just a journey through rugged landscapes; it is an immersive experience into the world of vertical descents, narrow slots, and breathtaking drops. It is an activity that combines hiking, scrambling, swimming, and technical rope work, presenting an exhilarating challenge for adventurers. Understanding the basics is crucial for those new to canyoneering before navigating Zion's intricate canyons. The essential gear includes a helmet, harness, ropes, and carabiners, each serving a critical function in ensuring safety throughout your adventure. Additionally, canyoneering shoes with a good grip and a wetsuit for colder water conditions are advisable. Skills such as rappelling, knot tying, and navigation are fundamental, typically acquired through proper training or guided outings. Zion offers numerous courses and guided tours that give beginners the necessary skills and confidence to tackle fundamental canyoneering challenges safely.

Navigating the permit system is essential in planning your canyoneering adventure in Zion. The park uses a lottery system for most of its canyoneering routes to manage the number of visitors and minimize environmental impact. Permits are required for all technical slot canyon routes and can either be reserved online through the park's website or obtained through a walk-in lottery at the visitor center. The online reservation system allows you to plan your trip months in advance, while the walk-in lottery is ideal for more spontaneous adventurers who might be flexible with their route choices. Understanding this system and planning is crucial, especially during peak seasons when demand for permits is high. This not only ensures your spot but also helps in preserving the pristine conditions of these natural wonders.

Figure 5 Zion National Park

The principles of eco-friendly exploration are vital in protecting the delicate ecosystems of Zion's canyons. The park's unique flora and fauna thrive in conditions easily disrupted by human activity. Stick to established paths to mitigate this and avoid trampling vegetation or disturbing wildlife. Pack out all trash and use biodegradable soap if washing is necessary. One of the most significant impacts of canyoneering is on the water systems within the canyons. To preserve these critical habitats, avoid introducing pollutants, including microfibers from clothing, which can accumulate and affect water quality. By adhering to these guidelines, you contribute to the conservation efforts that keep Zion's canyons as enchanting for future adventurers as they are today.

For those seeking solitude and untouched scenery, Zion harbors several lesser-known canyons that promise adventure away from the more frequented paths. Behunin Canyon offers a challenging yet rewarding experience with its rappels and stunning descents through narrow, water-carved walls. Though less visited, this canyon provides an intense full-day adventure for those with advanced canyoneering experience. Another hidden gem is Imlay Canyon, notorious for its difficulty and the technical skills it demands. Behunin Canyon is rarely visited due to its challenging obstacles, and thus, it remains one of the most pristine canyoneering experiences in the park. These off-the-beaten-path canyons are not for the faint-hearted but for those willing to endure; they offer unparalleled solitude and the raw beauty of Zion's wilderness, making the arduous journey entirely worthwhile. As you explore these remote areas, remember that their challenge matches the responsibility to maintain their untouched condition, ensuring they remain timeless in their rugged beauty.

1.6 Glacier National Park: Accessible Trails for All Abilities

Glacier National Park, known for its sweeping vistas and rugged mountain ranges, also offers a remarkable range of trails accessible to visitors of all abilities. Recognizing the importance of inclusivity in experiencing natural beauty, the park has developed a series of pathways that allow everyone, regardless of physical ability, to immerse themselves in its breathtaking environments. Among these, the Trail of the Cedars is an ideal starting point. This loop is flat and well-maintained and features a boardwalk that makes it navigable for wheelchairs and strollers. As you traverse this path, the ancient cedars and hemlocks envelop you, creating a serene atmosphere that heightens the sensory experience of the forest's subtle sounds and smells. Another accessible trail, the Sun Point Nature Trail, offers a short, scenic route with minimal elevation gain and spectacular views of St. Mary Lake and its surrounding peaks. Here, visitors can gaze across the water to the rugged outlines of Rising Wolf Mountain, often mirrored in the lake's still blue waters under the vast Montana sky.

Figure 6 Glacier National Park

Accessibility extends beyond the trails to the very services offered within the park. Shuttle services are available, equipped with lifts to assist those who need help boarding, ensuring that transportation within the park is not a barrier to exploration. These shuttles make several stops at prominent park attractions, including accessible viewpoints and picnic areas, allowing everyone to enjoy the park's renowned scenic spots without requiring extensive walking or hiking. Visitor centers, too, are fully accessible, providing a wealth of information through exhibits that are placed at appropriate heights and include audio descriptions and tactile models. Knowledgeable Park Rangers staff these centers, ready to assist visitors in planning their day in the park, ensuring that each person's needs and interests are met.

Engaging with nature in Glacier National Park is an experience that transcends physical limitations. The park's approach to accessibility ensures that all visitors, regardless of their mobility levels, can have meaningful and enriching interactions with the natural world. For instance, the Apgar Nature Center offers interactive programs to engage the senses beyond sight. Through these programs, visitors can touch various natural objects, listen to the park's sounds, and even smell different plants and minerals in the park. These activities are enjoyable and educational, providing insights into the park's ecosystem in a manner that is accessible to all. Additionally, ranger-led tours designed to accommodate visitors with limited mobility often take place on flat, easy trails or are conducted in seated areas with spectacular views, making it possible for everyone to learn about the park's history, wildlife, and geology.

Inclusivity in outdoor spaces like Glacier National Park represents a commitment to ensuring that the splendors of nature are available to all. This commitment is evident in the continuous efforts to maintain and improve the accessibility of the park's facilities and services. Glacier National Park is a beacon of inclusivity, from wheelchair-accessible trails to sensory-rich educational programs, inviting everyone to explore and connect with the great outdoors. As visitors of all abilities journey through its landscapes, they witness the majestic beauty of the natural world and participate in a shared experience emphasizing the universal value of nature's wonders. In this way, Glacier National Park enriches individual lives and fosters a collective appreciation for the environment and the importance of preserving it for future generations to experience and enjoy.

Chapter 2: The Coastal and Tropical Treasures

Picture yourself gliding through water so clear that every stroke of your paddle stirs up a deep history of thousands of years. As the mangroves whisper with the gentle ebb and flow of the tides, you find yourself at the heart of Everglades National Park—a mosaic of marine, estuarine, and terrestrial ecosystems that seamlessly weave together to form a sanctuary like no other. This chapter beckons you to dip your paddle into the glassy waters of the Everglades and navigate through its winding waterways, where every turn reveals the raw beauty of Florida's wilderness and the delicate balance of life that calls this place home.

2.1 Kayaking in Everglades National Park: A Water Adventure

Kayaking in the Everglades opens a world of adventure where the water's surface reflects the vast sky, and the sounds of nature play a symphony that resonates with the explorer's soul. For those who seek to experience this natural wonder, a variety of kayaking routes are available, each offering a unique perspective of the park's diverse landscapes. Novice kayakers might start with the Nine-Mile Pond trail. The trail meanders through calm waters, offering a gentle introduction to kayaking while soaking in the spectacular views of marshes and mangroves. More experienced paddlers might seek the challenge of the Turner River, where the route takes you through narrow, twisting passages that test your maneuvering skills amidst a dense canopy of mangroves. For the intrepid adventurer, the Wilderness Waterway will not disappoint; this 99-mile journey demands skill and perseverance, leading you from Everglades City to Flamingo through the heart of the park's backcountry.

One of the most exhilarating aspects of kayaking in the Everglades is the chance to encounter its diverse wildlife. The park is a sanctuary for many species, from the American crocodile basking on a muddy bank to the elusive Florida panther that might grace you with a rare appearance. Bird enthusiasts will be thrilled by the sight of ospreys diving for fish or the soft cooing of a Roseate Spoonbill. As you glide silently through the water, keep your eyes peeled and movements gentle to observe these creatures in their natural habitat. Maintaining a respectful distance, especially around nesting or hunting animals, is crucial to avoid disturbing their natural behaviors. A good pair of binoculars can enhance your experience, allowing you to watch wildlife from afar without intrusion.

Figure 7 Kayaking in Everglades National Park

Kayakers play a pivotal role in the conservation of the Everglades. As you paddle through these waters, you become a steward of its preservation. The park's ecosystems are susceptible to changes in water quality and flow, challenges exacerbated by broader environmental issues like climate change and urban development. By practicing eco-friendly kayaking, you contribute to the health of these ecosystems. Always follow the Leave No Trace principles—pack out what you bring in, avoid trampling over vegetation, and stay on designated water trails. Furthermore, participating in guided tours led by knowledgeable park rangers or local naturalists can deepen your understanding of the Everglades' ecological complexities and the critical conservation efforts underway to protect this unique environment.

Essential Safety Tips for Kayaking in the Everglades

Preparation is needed for a safe and enjoyable kayaking experience in the Everglades. Before setting out, check the weather conditions; the park's weather can be unpredictable, with sudden thunderstorms that can challenge even the most experienced kayakers. Always wear a life jacket, regardless of your swimming proficiency. Pack sunscreen, insect repellent, and plenty of water to stay hydrated under the Florida sun. Given the remoteness of many kayaking routes, a detailed map and a compass or GPS device are indispensable for navigation. Lastly, inform someone of your travel plans and expected return time, as cell service can be patchy in more isolated park areas.

As you embark on your kayaking adventure in the Everglades, embrace the opportunity to explore one of America's most unique national parks from the vantage point of its waters. Here, in the tranquil solitude of nature, you connect not just with the wild around you but also with the pulse of life that flows through this watery realm. Every paddle stroke carries you deeper into the heart of the Everglades, revealing the intricate beauty and profound importance of preserving such a treasure.

2.2 Olympic National Park: From Mountains to Tide Pools

Olympic National Park is a treasure trove of natural wonders and diverse landscapes, offering many attractions and activities for visitors. The park boasts lush temperate rainforests, such as the Hoh Rain Forest, where visitors can hike among towering trees draped in moss and ferns. For those seeking coastal adventures, the rugged Pacific coastline, with its dramatic sea stacks and tide pools, provides breathtaking views and opportunities for exploration. The park is also home to alpine regions like Hurricane Ridge, where panoramic vistas of snow-capped peaks and wildflower meadows await. Outdoor enthusiasts can enjoy various activities, including hiking, backpacking, camping, and wildlife watching, with the chance to spot species like Roosevelt elk and black bears. Additionally, the park's numerous rivers and lakes offer excellent opportunities for fishing, kayaking, and canoeing. With its rich biodiversity and stunning scenery, Olympic National Park is a haven for nature lovers and adventure seekers.

Figure 8 Olympic National Park

Exploring the Tidepools

Figure 9 Tide pools of Olympic National Park

Nestled within the rugged Pacific coastlines, the tide pools are natural aquariums teeming with life and color. These shallow pools of seawater, which remain after the tide recedes, provide a glimpse into the intricate marine ecosystems, highlighting a variety of species from sea stars to anemones. When exploring these fragile ecosystems, it is crucial to tread lightly and respect the life that thrives within them. The etiquette for tide pool exploration starts with your approach—walking gently around the edges of the tide pools rather than through them helps preserve the delicate balance of these ecosystems. It is also essential to remember that these environments are beautiful and vital for the survival of the species that inhabit them. Avoid picking up creatures or moving rocks, as this can disrupt their habitats. Observing with your eyes, not your hands, allows these ecosystems to flourish and continue to be a source of wonder for future visitors.

Identifying the most vibrant tide-pooling spots in Olympic National Park can transform your visit into an unforgettable exploration of marine biodiversity. Beach 4 and Rialto Beach are renowned for their accessible tide pools and the diversity of marine life they support. These locations are favored not only for their beauty but for the ease with which visitors can view sea life up close without venturing too far into sensitive areas. During low tide, the receding waters reveal pools that sparkle with life. Starfish cling to rocks in a mosaic of colors, while hermit crabs scuttle across the sandy bottoms, and mussels form clusters that adhere to the rugged coastline. Each pool provides a snapshot of the complex interdependencies that define these ecosystems, offering endless opportunities for discovery and learning.

For those keen to understand and identify the myriad species in these pools, a basic knowledge of tide pool marine life significantly enhances the experience. The Ochre Sea Star, a familiar yet striking inhabitant of these pools, can be seen in various hues from deep purple to bright orange. Green sea anemones, with their radiant tentacles, often carpet the rocky areas of the pools, creating a vivid underwater landscape. Look closer; you might spot the elusive sea cucumber or a small octopus hiding beneath a rock. Each species plays a pivotal role in the ecosystem, and learning to identify them adds a layer of appreciation for the complexity and resilience of these marine communities. Carrying a waterproof identification guide or using a mobile app dedicated to marine life can enrich your understanding and make your exploration more rewarding.

Understanding tides is crucial for anyone planning to explore the tide pools. The patterns of the tides dictate the accessibility and visibility of the tide pools, with low tide offering the best conditions for exploration. Before planning your visit, checking the local tide charts ensures you arrive at the optimal time to experience these ecosystems fully. Moreover, being aware of the tide schedule is a critical safety measure. The tides can change swiftly, and what was once a dry rock can quickly become an island as the tide rises. Always watch the water's edge and have a clear path back to higher ground. This awareness ensures a safe tide pooling experience and instills a more profound respect for the ocean's rhythms and the transient nature of the tide pools you are exploring. As you navigate these ephemeral landscapes, your mindful observations and interactions play a direct role in preserving and appreciating one of nature's most delicate marvels.

2.3 Hawaii Volcanoes National Park: Lava Viewing Tips and Safety

At Hawaii Volcanoes National Park, the primal force of Earth's creation unfolds before your eyes, presenting a rare opportunity to witness the dynamic transformation of the landscape through volcanic activity. The park offers a variety of viewpoints that allow you to safely observe the mesmerizing flow of lava as it reshapes the earth. The Jaggar Museum Overlook affords panoramic views of the Kīlauea Caldera and Halemaʻumaʻu Crater, often active with volcanic gases and occasional lava lake appearances that illuminate the night sky with a fiery glow. For a closer view of surface lava flows, when conditions permit, the areas along Chain of Craters Road provide a vantage point where the slow-moving lava meets the ocean, sending up plumes of steam and adding new land to the island's shores. These viewing spots are strategically positioned to offer safe and spectacular experiences. Still, it is crucial to stay within designated areas as the park officials continuously monitor volcanic activity and safety conditions.

Volcanic areas, while stunning, pose unique hazards; understanding these is critical for a safe visit. Volcanic gases, such as sulfur dioxide, can be hazardous to health, especially those with respiratory issues. It is important to heed all warning signs and ranger advice concerning gas emissions. The ground near active lava flows can be exceedingly unstable; newly formed crust over lava might look solid but can be dangerously thin. Keeping a safe distance from active lava flows is essential to avoid severe burns or other injuries. Additionally, changes in wind direction can quickly bring volcanic smog, or "vog," reducing air quality and visibility, which can affect driving and breathing. Staying informed through the park's visitor center updates and carrying a map of the area are steps to navigate these risks effectively.

Figure 10 Halema'uma'u Crater

The volcanoes of Hawaii are deeply embedded in the native Hawaiian culture, regarded not only as natural features but as sacred embodiments of the gods. Pele, the goddess of fire, who Native Hawaiians believe resides in Kīlauea, and many cultural traditions and practices are associated with her and the volcanic landscapes. Respecting these cultural beliefs is paramount when visiting the park. This includes observing any kapu (sacred) signs, not removing rocks or sand from the park, and being mindful of your actions and behaviors in these sacred areas. Participating in guided cultural tours can enrich your understanding of the significance of these volcanoes in Hawaiian culture, offering insights that transform your visit from a scenic tour to a profound, respectful engagement with the land and its ancestral ties.

Capturing the dramatic beauty of lava through photography is a popular activity, but it requires preparation and respect for safety guidelines. A superior quality camera with a zoom lens allows you to take stunning photos from a safe distance while avoiding getting too close to hazardous areas. Nighttime provides dramatic lighting conditions to photograph lava; however, it also presents challenges in terms of exposure and safety. Using a tripod can stabilize your camera for long exposures, capturing the vibrant glows of lava against the dark surroundings. Always ensure your camera equipment is secured and you stand on stable ground, as the terrain near volcanic activity can be unpredictable. Moreover, keeping a flashlight handy helps you find your way in the dark and makes you visible to others. By following these guidelines, your photography can capture the awe-inspiring nature of volcanic activity without compromising your safety or the integrity of the park's landscapes.

2.4 Channel Islands: Snorkeling and Marine Life Conservation

The Channel Islands, often called North America's Galapagos, offer a vibrant underwater world that remains one of the best-kept secrets in marine exploration. The isolation of these islands has preserved a unique ecosystem that thrives both above and below the water's surface. Among the kelp forests and rocky reefs, snorkelers can immerse themselves in an aquatic ballet of swirling fish, undulating sea plants, and the occasional curious seal. The clarity of the water here enhances visibility, making this a prime location for those who wish to delve into the marine world without the encumbrance of scuba gear.

The best spots for snorkeling in the Channel Islands vary based on what you wish to see and experience. For beginners, the protected waters of Scorpion Anchorage on Santa Cruz Island provide a safe and shallow environment with abundant marine life and easy beach access. More experienced snorkelers might seek the challenges and rewards of the outer islands like San Miguel, where Point Bennett offers a chance to observe larger marine species in deeper waters. Here, the interaction with playful pinnipeds and the glimpse of migrating whales enhances the thrill of the exploration. Regardless of your location, each dip into these waters promises a new discovery, as the cold currents that sweep through the islands nurture a rich diversity of life, from bright orange Garibaldi fish to elusive octopuses that blend into the rocky seabed.

Snorkelers' responsibility to contribute to conserving this pristine environment cannot be overstated. A commitment to minimal impact practices should guide every marine habitat visit to the Channel Islands. This includes avoiding contact with the sensitive kelp forest canopies, which are crucial nurseries for young fish. Maintaining a respectful distance from sea life, mainly seals and sea lions, is essential, as they can be stressed by close human interaction. Participating in conservation initiatives, such as citizen science projects that track sea conditions and marine life health, can also enhance the protection of these ecosystems. By documenting sightings of specific species or changes in the environment, snorkelers can provide valuable data that helps scientists and conservationists monitor the health of marine populations and the impact of human activities on these fragile ecosystems.

Snorkeling equipment must be carefully selected to ensure comfort and safety during underwater adventures around the Channel Islands. A well-fitting mask is crucial for clear visibility and to avoid water leakage. Snorkels with a purge valve reduce the effort needed to clear water from the tube, a handy feature in the choppy waters around the islands. Fins should be neither tight nor loose, as improperly fitting fins can lead to cramps or blisters that cut your exploration short. Wearing a wetsuit provides insulation in the cooler Pacific waters and protects against abrasions from rocks or accidental encounters with marine life like jellyfish. Lastly, always carry a diving knife and a whistle; these safety tools can be vital in unexpected situations, such as becoming entangled in discarded fishing lines or needing to signal your boat in an emergency. With the right gear and a respectful approach, snorkeling in the Channel Islands transforms into a safe and enriching experience, connecting you with the ocean's wonders in a way few other activities can match. As you float above the vibrant undersea landscapes, each breath through your snorkel and each kick of your fins brings you closer to understanding the intricate connections that sustain these aquatic communities, fostering a more profound commitment to their preservation.

2.5 Acadia National Park: Cycling the Carriage Roads

Nestled on the rugged coast of Maine, Acadia National Park offers a unique charm with its blend of dense forests, rocky beaches, and granite peaks. Among its many treasures, the carriage roads hold a special allure for cyclists seeking a physical challenge and a serene escape into nature. These historic paths, totaling forty-five miles, weave through the heart of the park, offering a network of routes explicitly designed without the interference of motor vehicles. The loop around Jordan Pond, the most scenic of these routes, provides stunning views of the Bubbles, twin hills standing guard over the pond's northern shore. As you pedal along, the fragrance of balsam firs fills the air, and the soft sounds of nature—a distant loon call or the rustle of deer through the underbrush—accompany your journey. Another popular route is the Eagle Lake loop, a slightly more challenging track that rewards cyclists with breathtaking vistas of one of the park's largest lakes, framed by mountains.

Figure 11 Acadia National Park

The history of Acadia's carriage roads is as rich as the landscapes they traverse. Built by John D. Rockefeller Jr. between 1913 and 1940, these roads were designed to complement the island's natural beauty, allowing visitors to explore the park's interior in a way that minimized impact on the environment. Rockefeller, an avid equestrian, envisioned a network of roads free from automobiles where visitors could experience the park's beauty in peace. He oversaw the construction, ensuring that each path was carefully integrated with the landscape, using native materials to construct bridges and guardrails that blended seamlessly with the surroundings. Today, these roads stand as a testament to his vision, continuing to offer a tranquil and immersive travel experience away from the bustle of modern life.

Preparing for a cycling adventure on Acadia's carriage roads involves thoughtful preparation to ensure enjoyment and safety. Primarily, choosing the right bicycle is crucial. A hybrid or mountain bike is recommended, as they are well-suited to manage the crushed rock surface of the carriage roads. Before you set out, a thorough check of your bike's condition is essential—pay attention to tire pressure, brake function, and gear operation. Dressing in layers allows you to adapt to the variable weather conditions typical of coastal Maine, and packing rain gear is always a wise precaution. Additionally, a helmet is indispensable for safety. Along with your gear, bring enough water to stay hydrated and high-energy snacks to maintain your stamina throughout the ride. Given the limited cell service in some areas of the park, carrying a map of the carriage roads is a good idea to navigate the network of routes without relying on digital devices.

Advocating responsible cycling practices on the carriage roads is necessary for preserving their historical and natural integrity. As you enjoy the freedom of cycling through Acadia's landscapes, adhering to Leave No Trace principles tailored to cyclists is vital. Stick to the gravel paths to avoid eroding the surrounding terrain and disturbing wildlife habitats. When encountering other park visitors, whether hikers, horseback riders, or fellow cyclists, practicing courteous trail etiquette ensures a pleasant experience for everyone. This includes communicating clearly when passing and maintaining a safe speed for the varied user groups enjoying the roads. Whatever you carry into the park—food wrappers, water bottles, or other personal items—should leave with you. Disposing of waste properly or packing it out helps maintain the pristine condition of the park for fellow adventurers and future generations.

2.6 Virgin Islands National Park: Sustainable Tourism and Coral Reefs

Nestled in the heart of the Caribbean, Virgin Islands National Park is a vibrant tapestry of blue waters, lush green hills, and coral reefs teeming with life. Here, the harmonious interplay of natural beauty and cultural heritage offers a unique opportunity for visitors to engage in sustainable tourism, directly contributing to the conservation of this precious ecosystem while immersing themselves in the local culture.

Embracing sustainable practices during your visit is crucial in preserving the park's natural and cultural resources. Simple actions can make a significant difference, such as choosing eco-friendly accommodations that adhere to green practices or opting for guided tours led by local experts knowledgeable about the park's ecosystems and cultural significance. These choices support local businesses and ensure that tourism positively impacts the community. Additionally, minimizing your use of single-use plastics helps reduce ocean pollution, a critical factor in maintaining the health of marine environments. When exploring the park, whether on land or at sea, always stick to marked trails and designated areas to prevent damage to fragile habitats and respect wildlife sanctuaries.

The coral reefs of Virgin Islands National Park are not just breathtaking natural wonders; they are also vital to the marine ecosystem, providing habitat, food, and protection for countless marine species. The health of these reefs is a delicate balance, influenced by both natural and human factors. Visitors can proactively participate in coral reef conservation by adhering to responsible snorkeling and diving practices. This includes maintaining proper buoyancy to avoid contact with the coral, which can be easily damaged. Touching or standing on coral harms the coral and can lead to infections or disease outbreaks within the reef community. It is also vital to use reef-safe sunscreen, as chemicals found in traditional sunscreens can cause coral bleaching and contribute to the degradation of these ecosystems.

Engaging with the local culture and community profoundly enriches your visit to Virgin Islands National Park. The islands have a rich cultural history influenced by Indigenous peoples, European colonialism, and African heritage, reflected in the local music, art, and festivals. Participating in cultural events or visiting local art galleries helps support the local economy and fosters a greater appreciation for the community's efforts to preserve their heritage. Moreover, many local conservation initiatives, such as beach clean-ups or educational programs, welcome visitor participation, providing firsthand opportunities to contribute to environmental stewardship efforts. By actively participating in these community and conservation activities, you enhance your experience and contribute to the sustainable development of the islands.

In summary, Virgin Islands National Park offers a perfect blend of natural beauty and cultural richness, making it an ideal destination for those seeking a sustainable travel experience. Visitors can actively preserve the park's unique environment and cultural heritage by adopting eco-friendly practices, respecting the delicate coral ecosystems, and engaging with the local community. This approach ensures the conservation of the park's resources and enriches the visitor experience, creating lasting memories and a deeper connection to this idyllic Caribbean paradise.

As we close this chapter on sustainable tourism and preserving coral reefs in the Virgin Islands National Park, we prepare to voyage further into the realms of America's national parks. Each park offers a gateway to explore extraordinary landscapes and diverse ecosystems and presents opportunities for personal growth and environmental responsibility. Whether gazing at the dynamic geysers of Yellowstone or trekking the rugged trails of the Grand Tetons, every experience is a step toward a more profound awareness and appreciation of our natural world. Join us in the next chapter as we explore these magnificent landscapes, each telling a story of beauty, resilience, and hope.

Chapter 3: The Heartlands and the Mountains

As the morning mist disperses, revealing the ancient Appalachian Mountains, you step into the enchanting world of the Smoky Mountains. This realm, where nature thrives under the canopy of one of America's most diverse ecosystems, is a living symphony of colors and life. The vibrant wildflowers and the secretive movements of wildlife paint a picture of a world waiting to be explored. Every path is a gateway to discovery, inviting you to delve into the rich biodiversity and deep-rooted culture that intertwine through the hills and valleys of this majestic landscape.

3.1 The Smoky Mountains: Seasonal Wildflowers and Wildlife

Wildflower Blooms: When and where to find the most spectacular wildflower displays.

The Smoky Mountains are often fondly referred to as the "Wildflower National Park," thanks to the prolific blooms that decorate the landscape through the seasons. Starting in late winter, you can witness the delicate beauty of trilliums, which pave the forest floor with white blossoms. As the season progresses into spring, the diversity explodes with vibrant displays of lady slipper orchids, lupines, and fiery flame azaleas. To experience these spectacular blooms, the Chestnut Top Trail is renowned for its spring wildflowers, offering a riot of colors that change weekly. Another notable path, the Gregory Bald Trail, is particularly famous for its azalea blooms in June, where the flowers paint the landscape in shades of orange, red, and gold. These trails offer a visual feast and a deep connection with nature's cycles, reminding us of the fleeting beauty that each season brings.

Figure 12 The Smoky Mountains

Wildlife Viewing: Tips for observing the park's wildlife respectfully and safely.

Home to abundant wildlife, the Smoky Mountains offer opportunities to observe animals in their natural habitats. From the majestic elk reintroduced to the park in the early 2000s to the stealthy bobcats and the playful otters, wildlife viewing can be a rewarding experience if done with respect and caution. Cades Cove and Cataloochee Valley are prime spots for viewing larger mammals, especially when animals are most active at dawn and dusk. While getting close for a better look or a photo is tempting, maintaining a safe distance is crucial to avoid disturbing the animals. Use binoculars or a zoom lens to enjoy detailed views without encroaching on their space. Keeping food secure and trash disposed of properly is also essential to prevent attracting wildlife to human areas, thereby keeping both animals and visitors safe.

Seasonal Activities: Highlighting different activities available throughout the seasons.

Each season in the Smokies unveils unique activities that cater to the adventurous spirit. Spring's mild weather is perfect for hiking and enjoying the abundant wildflowers. Summer offers lush greenery and the cool retreats of mountain streams, ideal for fishing or cooling off.

Come autumn, the landscape turns into a canvas of breathtaking fall colors, perfect for scenic drives or photography. Winter, though quieter, brings the frosty beauty of snow-covered paths, suitable for cross-country skiing or snowshoeing. The park also hosts various seasonal events, such as the Spring Wildflower Pilgrimage and the Fall Harvest Festival, which celebrate the natural and cultural heritage of the Smokies, offering guided tours, workshops, and family-friendly activities.

Conservation Messages: How visitors can contribute to the preservation of the Smokies' natural beauty

Preserving the natural beauty and biodiversity of the Smoky Mountains is a collective responsibility that extends to all who visit. The park's efforts in conservation are supported by the cooperation of guests who adhere to eco-friendly practices. Staying on designated trails prevents soil erosion and protects plant life. Participating in the park's recycling programs and avoiding single-use plastics helps minimize waste. Additionally, volunteering for trail maintenance or joining educational programs can enrich your understanding of the park's ecosystems and the importance of protecting them. By engaging in these practices, you contribute to the conservation efforts that ensure the Smokies remain a haven for future generations to explore and cherish.

As you delve deeper into the heartlands and mountains, each step through the Smoky Mountains connects you with the tranquility of nature and the ongoing efforts to preserve these landscapes. The delicate balance of enjoying and conserving the environment ensures that the wonders of the Smokies continue to inspire and nurture all who wander through its paths.

3.2 Rocky Mountain National Park: High Altitude Hiking Tips

Acclimatization Advice: Preparing for high altitude hikes to avoid altitude sickness.

As you set your sights on the peaks of Rocky Mountain National Park, understanding and preparing for the altitude is required. The park's trails reach elevations where the air is thinner and oxygen is less abundant, making acclimatization a necessity for the enjoyment and safety of your hike. Starting your adventure with a plan to acclimate gradually can significantly enhance your experience. Spend a few days at a moderate elevation near the park before attempting higher climbs. This adjustment period helps your body adapt to lower oxygen levels, reducing the potential for altitude sickness. Additionally, keeping hydrated is more important than ever at high altitudes. The dry air and exertion can lead to dehydration, exacerbating symptoms of altitude sickness such as headaches, nausea, and dizziness. Drink plenty of water and include electrolyte-replenishing beverages in your hydration plan. Another tip is to take it slow, pace yourself, and allow your body to acclimate as you ascend. Listening to your body is essential; it is wise to rest or descend to a lower altitude at any sign of discomfort.

Trail Selection: Choosing trails that match your fitness level and altitude experience.

Selecting the right trail in Rocky Mountain National Park is not just about matching physical fitness but also considering your experience with altitude. For those new to high-altitude hiking, start with trails that offer gradual ascents. The Bear Lake area provides a variety of such trails, ranging from strolls around the lake to more challenging hikes up to Flattop Mountain. Each trail offers opportunities to gauge your response to the altitude without committing to a strenuous climb. For seasoned high-altitude hikers, the park provides more ambitious treks, such as the ascent to Longs Peak, a demanding hike that rewards the hiker with expansive views from the summit. Before choosing a trail, review detailed trail maps available at park visitor centers. Check the elevation gain and trail length, and realistically assess your current fitness level and acclimatization. Remember, the goal is to enjoy the journey as much as the destination, and selecting the right trail is a big part of that enjoyment.

Figure 13 Rocky Mountain National Park

Weather Preparedness: Navigating the quickly changing weather conditions at high altitudes.

Rocky Mountain National Park weather can change rapidly, transforming a clear morning into a challenging afternoon of wind and snow. Such shifts are especially pronounced at higher elevations, where weather conditions can be more extreme and less predictable. A key strategy to navigate these changes safely is to start your hikes early in the day. Afternoon thunderstorms are common in mountainous areas, particularly in summer, so an early start can help you descend before storms develop. Equipping yourself with the right gear is also vital. Always carry a waterproof jacket, extra layers for warmth, and sun protection, including sunscreen and a hat. A compact emergency shelter, such as a space blanket or bivy sack, can be a lifesaver if caught in an unexpected storm. Additionally, keep an eye on the sky and be ready to turn back if the weather looks like it is turning. Many hikers use weather apps or portable weather radios to keep updated on forecasts, a practice that can provide critical information when you are far from a shelter.

Impact Reduction: Strategies to minimize environmental impact while hiking in sensitive areas.

Hiking in Rocky Mountain National Park offers recreation and the responsibility to protect the fragile alpine environments you explore. Minimizing your impact starts with sticking to marked trails to avoid trampling alpine vegetation, which can be incredibly slow to recover in the harsh high-altitude climate. When hiking, use durable surfaces such as rock, gravel, or dry grasses to rest or camp, avoiding areas where impact on vegetation can occur. Campfires can cause lasting damage in these sensitive environments, so use a lightweight stove for cooking and enjoy natural night skies instead of a fire. Pack out all your trash and use established restrooms, or carry a portable waste system if you are venturing into areas without facilities. Another way to reduce your impact is to hike in smaller groups, as large groups tend to have a higher environmental impact and can also detract from the wilderness experience for others. By embracing these practices, you preserve the park's natural beauty and ensure it remains a pristine sanctuary for future generations to enjoy.

3.3 Badlands National Park: Otherworldly Geology and Stargazing

The Badlands National Park, known for its striking geological formations and expansive sky views, offers a landscape that feels like one has stepped onto another planet. The park's rugged beauty is sculpted from sedimentary rock layers shaped by water and wind over millions of years. These layers tell a vivid story of the Earth's geological past, displaying distinct bands of color that reveal different environmental conditions and the passage of time. The formations include sharply eroded buttes, pinnacles, and spires that defy easy description and inspire awe with their dramatic appearances. To genuinely appreciate the complexity of these geological features, a visit to the Door Trail is essential. A boardwalk leads through a break in the Badlands Wall, offering close-up views of the intricately eroded rock formations. The trail allows you to witness the results of natural forces at work and provides interpretive panels that explain the geological processes that have shaped the landscape. Understanding how these formations came to be enhances the appreciation of their beauty and the natural forces that continue to sculpt them.

The park's unique geological features also create an ideal backdrop for stargazing. With minimal light pollution and an open horizon, the Badlands offer some of the darkest night skies in the United States. The Sage Creek Basin is one of the prime spots for astronomers and night sky enthusiasts. This area provides a panoramic sky view, allowing for unobstructed observation of celestial events. Whether you are watching a meteor shower, identifying constellations, or observing the milky band of the Milky Way, the experience is enhanced by the stark silhouette of the Badlands formations under the night sky. For those interested in guided experiences, the park offers night sky viewing programs, including telescope observations facilitated by rangers. These programs provide the equipment necessary for deep sky viewing and offer expert insights into the stars and planets that light up the night sky.

Fossil hunting in the Badlands offers another layer of adventure, connecting you with the ancient life forms that once inhabited this land. The park is one of the richest fossil beds in the world, home to well-preserved remains of ancient mammals such as the saber-toothed cat. To engage in fossil hunting, it is crucial to do so responsibly and within the regulations set by the park. While visitors cannot collect fossils, you can join ranger-led programs that explore the fossil beds and offer opportunities to discover fossils in situ. These programs educate participants on the types of fossils found in the Badlands and the significance of these findings in understanding the region's prehistoric environment. These educational activities allow for a direct experience that respects the park's preservation efforts while providing a tangible connection to the Earth's ancient past.

Figure 14 Badlands National Park

Capturing the Badlands' stunning landscapes and night skies through photography offers a creative outlet to convey the beauty and otherworldliness of the park. The park's dramatic vistas and clear, starlit nights provide ideal conditions for photographers. To capture the textured landscape and sprawling vistas, consider using a wide-angle lens, which can embrace the vastness of the scenery and the scale of the geological formations. For night photography, a tripod is essential to stabilize your camera for long exposures, which is necessary to capture the faint light of stars. Experimenting with different shutter speeds and apertures can help find the perfect balance to illuminate the night sky against the dark outlines of the land. Remember to respect the natural environment as you set up your equipment, staying on designated paths and areas to minimize your impact on the fragile terrain. Photography in the Badlands allows you to preserve memories of your visit and share the park's unique landscape with others, inspiring appreciation and conservation of these natural wonders.

3.4 The Caves of Wind Cave National Park: Underground Exploration

Deep beneath the rolling prairies of South Dakota lies one of the world's most complex cave systems, Wind Cave National Park. Known for its rare boxwork formations, this underground network offers a variety of tours that cater to different interests and abilities, making it an accessible adventure for many. For those new to cave exploration, the Garden of Eden tour provides an accessible introduction, featuring relatively flat paths and minimal stairs, allowing participants to admire the delicate crystalline structures without strenuous physical exertion. More adventurous souls might opt for the Fairgrounds Tour, which covers a longer distance and includes several stairs, offering a more comprehensive exploration of the cave's diverse environments. For the most daring, the Wild Cave Tour is a thrilling challenge that involves crawling through undeveloped cave sections. This physically demanding experience requires participants to wear protective gear and navigate through tight passages, offering an intimate encounter with the cave's raw beauty.

Preserving the pristine condition of Wind Cave is crucial to maintaining its natural beauty and protecting the delicate ecosystems that thrive in the underground environment. The cave's environment is extremely sensitive to temperature, humidity, and airflow changes, all of which can be impacted by human activity. As visitors explore the cave, sticking to marked paths and avoiding touching the formations is vital. The oils from human skin can disrupt the delicate mineral deposits that form the cave's features. Many tours educate participants about the importance of conservation, highlighting how each person's behavior can contribute to preserving this natural wonder. Additionally, the park participates in ongoing research and monitoring efforts to understand and mitigate human impacts, ensuring that the cave remains a sustainable attraction for future generations.

When planning for a cave tour at Wind Cave National Park, knowing what to expect and how to prepare can significantly enhance your experience. Most tours require walking through dimly lit, often narrow, passages with varying temperatures and humidity levels. Wearing comfortable, non-slip shoes is essential, as cave floors can be wet and uneven. Dressing in layers can also help manage the cooler temperatures typically found underground, usually around 53 degrees Fahrenheit, regardless of the surface weather. A small, hands-free light source like a headlamp can be helpful, especially on the more adventurous tours where extra illumination is beneficial. Before your tour, it is also a good idea to familiarize yourself with the cave's safety guidelines, designed to protect both the cave environment and its visitors. These preparations ensure that your exploration of Wind Cave is enjoyable and respects the cave's natural state.

The cultural significance of Wind Cave extends far beyond its geological features. For the Lakota people, this cave is an important spiritual site, considered to be the location where their people first emerged into the world. The cave's natural entrance is known as the hole that blows air, aligning with Lakota stories that speak of a sacred breath or wind that signifies the passage between worlds. Understanding the cultural heritage of Wind Cave can transform your visit from a simple tour into a deeper appreciation of this sacred site. Many park rangers include stories of the Lakota people in their tours, providing insights into the traditional beliefs and the significance of the cave in Native American history. This integration of cultural heritage emphasizes the connection between the natural world and human history, enriching the visitor experience with a profound sense of place and tradition. As you walk through the twisting paths of Wind Cave, you are exploring a unique geological formation and a landscape steeped in centuries of spiritual significance, echoing the stories and beliefs of the Lakota people who have long revered this sacred site.

3.5 The Bison of Theodore Roosevelt National Park: Viewing with Respect

The rolling plains of Theodore Roosevelt National Park serve as a stage where the American bison, a symbol of wild heritage, plays a starring role. Observing these majestic creatures in their natural habitat offers a glimpse into the past, where bison roamed freely across vast expanses of the country. Understanding bison behavior is crucial for any visitor. Despite their often calm demeanor, these animals are unpredictable and can charge if threatened. Typically, bison spend much of their time grazing, moving slowly across grasslands, but during the rutting season, their behavior can become more aggressive as males vie for mates. During these times, maintaining a safe distance becomes even more critical. The park guidelines recommend staying at least twenty-five yards away from these large mammals; however, even greater distances may be advisable during the rut. Observing their body language helps gauge their mood; signs of agitation include snorting, pawing the ground, or lowering their heads. By respecting these signals, you ensure both your safety and their well-being, making your viewing experience both enjoyable and respectful.

Finding the best spots in the park for bison viewing and photography can enhance your visit significantly. The scenic loop drive in the park's South Unit offers numerous opportunities to see bison in their natural settings. This route takes you through prairie dog towns, which often attract bison. With its expansive views, the Painted Canyon area is another excellent location where bison are frequently spotted grazing along the colorful badlands. Early morning or late afternoon provides the best light for photography and is also when bison are most active, making these times ideal for visits. Positioning yourself with the sun behind you can lead to stunning photographic compositions, capturing the bison's iconic profile against the park's sweeping landscapes. Always use a good zoom lens to keep a respectful distance; this ensures safety and prevents the bison from being disturbed by your presence.

Figure 15 Bison in Theodore Roosevelt National Park

The conservation story of the bison in Theodore Roosevelt National Park is a powerful testament to successful wildlife management and recovery efforts. Once on the brink of extinction, with population numbers dwindling to just a few hundred in the late 1800s due to overhunting and habitat loss, the American bison has made a remarkable comeback. The park has played a crucial role in these conservation efforts. In the 1950s, a small herd of twenty-nine bison was reintroduced to the park, providing a secure environment for them to grow and thrive. Today, the park's bison population is a healthy and genetically diverse group, highlighting the success of these efforts. Regular health checks, genetic monitoring, and careful management of grazing areas help maintain the balance between the bison and their environment. This ongoing work ensures the stability of the ecosystem, supporting not just the bison but a myriad of other species that share their habitat.

Adhering to wildlife viewing etiquette is not just about safety; it reflects a profound respect for the natural world. When watching bison, use binoculars or camera zooms to enjoy close-up views without encroaching on their space. If you are driving and encounter bison on or near the road, remain in your vehicle and give them the right of way. The park's bison often use the roads as travel corridors, a behavior that can lead to memorable encounters right from the safety of your car. It is also essential to keep noise to a minimum to avoid causing stress to the bison. Refrain from feeding wildlife, which can alter their natural behaviors and diet. By following these simple guidelines, your experience in Theodore Roosevelt National Park not only becomes a highlight of your visit but also contributes to the ethos of conservation that the park upholds. This respectful engagement with nature ensures that the legacy of the American bison continues to be a source of inspiration and awe for all who step into this historic landscape.

3.6 Cuyahoga Valley National Park: A Historical Journey

Between the bustling urban areas of Cleveland and Akron, Cuyahoga Valley National Park offers a respite where history and nature intertwine along the meandering Cuyahoga River. This park serves as a green oasis and a living museum, displaying the rich tapestry of industrial and cultural history that has shaped the region. Exploring its historical sites, you travel in time, where each landmark tells a story of the past, from Native American tribes to the rise and fall of Ohio's canal era.

One of the must-visit historical sites within the park is the Hale Farm & Village, a living history museum that transports you back to the mid-19th century. Here, you can explore restored farm buildings, craft workshops, and gardens, each staffed by costumed interpreters who demonstrate daily life and crafts from the era. Another pivotal site is the Everett Covered Bridge, the only remaining covered bridge in the park, which recalls a time when such structures were vital for crossing Cuyahoga's often treacherous waters. This bridge serves as a picturesque reminder of the past and tells the story of community and connectivity in the valley. Also, a visit to the remnants of the Ohio & Erie Canal offers a glimpse into the transformative period when the canal served as a crucial transportation route that spurred economic growth and settlement in the region.

Engaging in eco-friendly tourism practices while exploring the Cuyahoga Valley emphasizes a respectful and sustainable interaction with this historical landscape. The park's commitment to sustainability is evident in its efforts to preserve natural resources while accommodating visitors. You can partake in these efforts by utilizing the park's recycling facilities, adhering to designated trails to prevent soil erosion, and participating in guided tours that educate on the park's ecology and conservation projects. The Ledges Trail, for example, offers breathtaking views of the valley's unique rock formations and features interpretive signs that explain the geological history and the importance of preserving such landmarks. By engaging with the park in these mindful ways, you contribute to the ongoing efforts to balance conservation with public enjoyment and education.

The park comes alive with various seasonal events celebrating its cultural heritage and natural beauty. The fall Heritage Series, for example, highlights traditional arts, crafts, and music, offering workshops and performances that reflect the valley's historical roots. Spring brings the annual Cuyahoga Valley Birding Festival, a celebratory event that underscores the park's role as a habitat for migratory birds, featuring guided bird walks and educational talks. These events not only enhance the visitor experience but also foster a greater appreciation for the park's cultural and natural resources, reinforcing the connection between the community and the preservation of its historical and ecological heritage.

Trails in Cuyahoga Valley do more than traverse scenic landscapes; they lead you through the pages of history. The Ohio & Erie Canal Towpath

Trail, once a route for mules towing canal boats, now serves as a pathway that offers not only leisure and exercise but also educational insight into the area's development. As you walk, bike, or ride along this trail, you are following in the footsteps of the past, with access to historical sites and interpretive displays that enrich your understanding of the valley's transformation over the centuries. Similarly, the Brandywine Falls Trail presents a stunning natural waterfall, while nearby, the restored Brandywine Grist Mill adds historical context to the region's once-thriving milling industry.

As this chapter closes on Cuyahoga Valley National Park, we reflect on the dynamic interaction between nature and history that defines this unique national treasure. The journey through its landscapes is a testament to the enduring spirit of preservation and education that guides the National Park Service. Each trail and event celebrates and protects the cultural and natural heritage of this vital part of Ohio. As we turn our gaze forward, the exploration continues, promising more stories to uncover and more wonders to behold in the next chapter of America's national parks.

Chapter 4: The Desert Landscapes

Imagine standing amidst an expansive canvas where the earth stretches infinitely, painted with burnt orange, deep red, and golden yellow hues. Here, in the heart of the desert landscapes of America, each grain of sand tells a story of resilience and adaptation. Often perceived as a barren expanse, the desert reveals its true character through bursts of life and color that defy the harsh environment. It is a place where silence speaks volumes, and the air, though arid, carries whispers of ancient secrets waiting to be uncovered. As the sun rises, casting long shadows over the dunes, you are invited to explore these mystical terrains that offer more than meets the eye.

4.1 Death Valley's Superblooms: Nature's Resilience

Superbloom Phenomenon: Explaining the conditions that lead to a superbloom and when to visit.

In the inhospitable environment of Death Valley, a miraculous event unfolds with the arrival of a superbloom, turning the desert floor into a vibrant tapestry of colors. This rare phenomenon, where the valley bursts into full bloom with an array of wildflowers, occurs only under perfect conditions. Following seasons of significant rainfall, a hidden reservoir of seeds beneath the barren surface springs to life, carpeting the landscape in hues of gold, purple, pink, and white. The most common wildflowers include the golden evening primrose, desert gold, and the delicate purple phacelia. Timing your visit is crucial to witness this spectacle, typically possible from late February to early April, though this can vary based on the precipitation patterns of the winter months. The transformation of the desert during a superbloom is a poignant reminder of the resilience of life and the hidden potential lying dormant beneath the surface, awaiting the perfect conditions to emerge.

Figure 16 Death Valley Superbloom

Photography Tips: Capturing the vibrant beauty of the superbloom while minimizing environmental impact.

Photographing a superbloom in Death Valley is a unique opportunity to capture the contrast between the usual starkness of the desert and the brief explosion of life. However, it's crucial to remember that this is a delicate ecosystem. To photograph this event while preserving the integrity of the landscape, it is essential to tread lightly and respect the fragile blooms. Use a zoom lens to capture detailed images of the flowers without needing to step close and potentially damage the delicate plants. Employing a polarizing filter can help enhance the colors and reduce glare, bringing out the vivid details of the flowers against the dusty desert background. Always stick to established trails and viewing areas to avoid trampling the blooms. Remember, the goal is to leave no trace of your presence, ensuring the superbloom can be enjoyed by others and preserved for future seasons.

Visitor Etiquette: Guidelines for enjoying the superblooms without damaging the fragile ecosystem.

Experiencing a superbloom is a privilege that comes with responsibility. The desert ecosystem, despite its rugged appearance, is incredibly sensitive. Visitors are urged to follow strict guidelines to ensure their presence does not disturb this rare natural event. Staying on designated paths and areas is crucial; straying off can damage the soil and the plant life of the desert's fragile ecological network. It is also important to avoid picking flowers or collecting seeds, as this can affect the longevity and intensity of current and future blooms. By observing these simple acts of respect, you contribute to the sustainability of the superbloom phenomena, ensuring that these desert wonders continue to thrive and inspire.

Water Conservation: The importance of water conservation in desert environments and practical tips.

In the context of a desert, where every drop of water is precious, conservation becomes a critical practice. The survival of the desert's flora and fauna depends on efficiently using limited water resources, a balance easily disrupted by human activity. Visitors to desert parks like Death Valley are encouraged to conserve water by minimizing usage and avoiding activities that could lead to water contamination. Carrying reusable water containers, using water sparingly when camping or picnicking, and ensuring that all personal waste is correctly disposed of are simple yet effective ways to sustain the park's water integrity. Educating oneself about the desert's ecosystem and the role of water within it can also enhance one's appreciation for these environments, underscoring the importance of conservation efforts in preserving the natural beauty and ecological health of our desert landscapes.

As you venture through these arid regions, each step unveils the desert's stark beauty and enduring resilience. From the fleeting magnificence of a superbloom to the enduring silhouettes of ancient rock formations, these landscapes ask for respect and mindfulness from those who walk their sacred grounds. Here in the heart of the desert, you learn that life, no matter how fragile it seems, finds a way to assert itself with spectacular vibrancy, painting the canvas of the earth with strokes of survival and beauty.

4.2 Arches National Park: Photography Without Crowds

Figure 17 Arches National Park

Arches National Park's iconic landscape of contrasting colors, landforms, and textures offers photographers a canvas of extraordinary natural architecture. Yet, such beauty rarely remains uncrowded, making it a challenge to capture the serene solitude of the arches without interrupting fellow visitors. To experience and photograph Arches in its most undisturbed state, knowing a few lesser-known spots can significantly enhance your photographic journey. Beyond the frequently visited Delicate Arch or the Windows Section, the park harbors quieter locales such as Tower Arch in the Klondike Bluffs area. This lesser-trodden arch offers a grand yet solitary experience, ideal for photography. Another hidden gem is the Broken Arch at sunrise, which sees fewer visitors and presents an alignment with the rising sun that bathes the arch in warm, golden hues, perfect for dramatic light and shadow play in your compositions.

The timing of your photography expedition can make a substantial difference in both the quality of your images and the solitude of your experience. Capturing the majestic formations of Arches National Park requires understanding light and how it plays across the sandstone landscapes. Early morning light, just after sunrise, casts a gentle, diffuse glow that enhances the red rock formations with a soft, warm light ideal for photography. This time also tends to be quieter, as the crowds have yet to arrive. Conversely, late afternoon leading into sunset brings out the deep reds and shadows, offering a dramatic contrast and mood to your images. However, to avoid the typical sunset crowd at popular spots like Delicate Arch, consider positioning yourself at lesser-known north-facing arches during this golden hour. The sun's low angle illuminates the undersides of these arches, creating a magnificent natural glow for photography.

Practicing Leave No Trace photography is crucial in preserving Arches National Park's natural beauty and integrity. As a photographer, minimizing your impact on the environment is essential. This includes staying on designated paths and trails, as straying off can lead to soil erosion and damage to the cryptobiotic crust, a vital component of the desert ecosystem. When setting up tripods, ensure they are placed on durable surfaces such as rock or in areas already compacted by human activity. Avoid placing equipment on vegetation or undisturbed soil. Additionally, be mindful of the park's guidelines regarding the use of drones, as they are prohibited in National Parks. These practices ensure that the spectacular landscapes continue to thrive and remain photogenic for generations.

For those looking to deepen their photographic skills while exploring Arches, local photography workshops offer guided tours focusing on technique and ethical practices in nature photography. These workshops are typically led by experienced photographers familiar with the park's geography. They can take you to iconic and obscure locations, maximizing your experience across different lighting and weather conditions. They provide firsthand instruction on various aspects of landscape photography, from composition and lighting to advanced techniques like long exposure and HDR imaging. These workshops often include sessions on environmental awareness and the importance of conservation-minded photography, helping participants understand and implement practices that protect the park's natural beauty while capturing its essence. Engaging in a photography workshop in Arches National Park enhances your skills and enriches your appreciation for the delicate desert environment, making your photographic experience both rewarding and responsible.

4.3 Petrified Forest National Park: A Journey Through Time

The Petrified Forest National Park, stretching across northeastern Arizona, offers a vivid narrative of Earth's vibrant past, encapsulated within its landscapes strewn with the colorful remains of fossilized trees. This remarkable transformation, where wood becomes stone, unfolds over millions of years through permineralization. Here, mineral-rich water seeps into the porous wood, depositing minerals in the cells as lignin and cellulose decay. Over time, this process solidifies the wood into quartz, preserving the intricate details of the bark and the rings, thus recording a moment from the Late Triassic period, approximately 225 million years ago. This geological marvel provides a rare glimpse into the conditions of the past, where this now arid landscape was a lush, vibrant environment teeming with life. The park's unique terrain, characterized by the stark contrasts between the colorful badlands and the glittering petrified logs, is a testament to the dynamic forces of nature and time.

Figure 18 Petrified Forest National Park

For those eager to delve deeper into the world of ancient landscapes, the Petrified Forest offers extensive opportunities for fossil viewing. The park is renowned for its wealth of well-preserved fossils that provide insight into the late Triassic ecosystem. To engage in fossil viewing responsibly, it is vital to adhere to the guidelines provided by the park. While touching or taking pieces of petrified wood as souvenirs is tempting, such actions are prohibited. Instead, visitors are encouraged to use the marked trails and designated viewing areas where interpretive signs offer valuable information about the fossils. These paths are carefully planned to afford excellent views without compromising the site's integrity. For a more educational experience, consider joining a ranger-led tour, where experts share insights into the paleontological significance of the finds and the broader environmental history they suggest.

The Painted Desert, part of the larger Petrified Forest National Park, offers an otherworldly landscape of colorful stratified rock formations ranging from lavenders to reds, shaped by the forces of erosion. This stunning display of nature's artistry is best explored through the park's designated hiking trails, designed to minimize human impact while maximizing the visual feast. The Tawa Point trail offers panoramic views of the Painted Desert's expansive vistas, providing a perfect spot for sunrise or sunset when the colors shift and deepen. Hikers are reminded to prepare adequately for these excursions, as the desert environment can be unforgiving. Essential preparations include carrying plenty of water, wearing sun protection, and dressing in layers to adapt to the fluctuating temperatures. Staying on the marked trails is crucial for safety and protecting the fragile crust of the desert soil, which plays a critical role in preventing erosion and supporting the sparse desert vegetation.

Conservation efforts in Petrified Forest National Park are robust, focusing on protecting the geological and paleontological resources and ensuring that the park's natural beauty remains unspoiled for future generations. These efforts include ongoing research projects that study the fossils and the environmental conditions of the Triassic Period, providing deeper insights into climate patterns and ecological shifts. The park's management practices also emphasize the importance of sustainable tourism, which is critical in an environment as delicate as the desert. Initiatives such as limiting areas for vehicle access, creating designated picnic areas, and providing comprehensive educational programs about the desert ecosystem are all part of a broader strategy to foster environmental stewardship among visitors. By participating in these efforts and adhering to park regulations, visitors play an active role in conserving one of America's most unique national treasures, ensuring that its stories and splendors continue to inspire awe and curiosity well into the future.

Exploring Petrified Forest National Park immerses you in a narrative of transformation and endurance, where every stone and grain of sand has a story to tell. It is a place where the past is palpably present, inviting you to wander, wonder, and witness nature's enduring power in sculpting our planet's landscape. As you traverse this ancient terrain, you walk through chapters of Earth's history, each step a testament to the relentless passage of time and the transformative forces that shape our world.

4.4 Big Bend National Park: Stargazing and Solitude

Big Bend National Park, nestled in the remote reaches of West Texas, offers one of the most pristine night skies in the United States. Its location, far from the light pollution of major cities, makes it an ideal sanctuary for stargazing. Its International Dark Sky Park certification shows the park's commitment to preserving a dark sky. This designation is not just a title; it represents a commitment to adopting practices that minimize light pollution and educate visitors about the importance of dark skies. Nighttime in Big Bend opens a window to the universe, where the Milky Way stretches across the sky in a dazzling display of cosmic splendor. To support this preservation effort, visitors are encouraged to use only red lights for night navigation, as these have minimal impact on night vision and the overall dark sky environment. Participating in one of the park's ranger-led night sky programs can deepen your appreciation of the stars during your stay. These programs often include telescope viewing, where celestial objects are brought into stunning clarity, and discussions on how light pollution affects our view of the night sky and what steps can be taken to reduce it.

For those seeking solitude, Big Bend's expansive landscapes offer countless opportunities to find peace away from the crowds. The Outer Mountain Loop, for example, is a challenging trail that rewards hikers with incredible solitude and breathtaking views of the Chisos Mountains and the surrounding desert. This 30-mile trek requires preparation and resilience, attributes that are rewarded with moments of profound stillness and connection with nature. For a less demanding but equally rewarding experience, the Santa Elena Canyon Trail offers a shorter hike along the Rio Grande. Here, the towering canyon walls envelop you, creating a natural sanctuary where the sounds of the river and the rustle of the wind in the reeds are your only companions. These trails are more than just paths through the desert; they are passages into a more profound experience of solitude, where the vastness of the landscape provides a rare sense of scale and perspective.

Navigating the areas near the U.S.-Mexico border in Big Bend requires an awareness of safety and legal considerations. The park shares a 118-mile boundary with Mexico, marked in parts by the Rio Grande. While hiking near the border, it is essential always to carry proper identification, as Border Patrol agents may be operating in the area. Additionally, while incidents are rare, staying informed about the current travel advisories and park regulations regarding border safety is prudent. The park rangers are a valuable resource for the latest information and can provide tips on how to enjoy the border regions of the park safely. They can advise on which areas are best suited for visitors and any precautions to take when embarking on trails near the border.

Desert safety is paramount in Big Bend, where the harsh conditions demand respect and preparation. The desert climate can be unforgiving, with temperatures soaring during the day and dropping rapidly after sunset. Staying hydrated is critical; carry more water than you think you need and plan your hikes for early morning or late evening to avoid the midday heat. Sun protection, including a hat, sunscreen, and long sleeves, can help prevent sunburn and heat exhaustion. It is also wise to have a detailed map and a GPS, as some park areas have limited cell phone coverage. Understanding the signs of heat stroke and heat exhaustion can be lifesaving, as is knowing how to respond if symptoms appear. Finally, always let someone know your travel plans and expected return time, especially if you are venturing into remote areas of the park. These practices ensure that your exploration of Big Bend's stunning desert landscape is memorable and safe, allowing you to fully engage with the region's rugged beauty without undue risk.

4.5 Saguaro National Park: The Giants of the Desert

In the arid expanses of Saguaro National Park, the iconic saguaro cactus stands as a sentinel of the Sonoran Desert. These towering giants, reaching heights surpassing forty feet, symbolize the American Southwest and a vital part of the desert ecosystem. The lifecycle of a saguaro cactus is a marvel of nature's adaptability. Beginning as a tiny seed, no larger than a pinhead, it faces a survival challenge, as germination rates are low and conditions harsh. Those that do sprout may grow only an inch in their first six years, shadowed by nurse plants like palo verde or mesquite, which provide necessary shade and moisture conservation. As decades pass, these cacti develop their first arms, an iconic feature that can take up to 75 years to appear, signaling maturity and the beginning of their reproductive phase.

Figure 19 A Saguaro Cactus in Saguaro National Park

The saguaro's blooming season in late spring offers a spectacle where white, waxy flowers crown the tops of each trunk and arm, opening at night to invite pollination by nectar-loving bats, a perfect adaptation to the desert's nocturnal life. These flowers later give way to red, fleshy fruits, each bursting with up to 2,000 black seeds, thus continuing the life cycle in the desert. Saguaros can live more than two hundred years, becoming central figures in their habitat. They offer food through their fruits and flowers and provide homes for desert wildlife, including birds such as the Gila woodpecker and the elf owl, which nest in holes burrowed into the cactus flesh. This role underscores the saguaro's importance in fostering biodiversity and sustaining the ecological networks of the Sonoran Desert.

Photographing these majestic cacti requires patience and timing, particularly to capture the essence of their role within the desert landscape. Early mornings offer soft light that enhances the saguaro's texture and form against the stark desert backdrop. Utilizing the golden hours at sunrise or sunset can also dramatize the scene, casting long shadows or bathing the cactus in a warm glow that highlights its grandeur. A common technique is to use a low angle and a wide-angle lens to convey the imposing height and stature of the saguaro, providing a sense of scale by including familiar elements, such as a human figure or a common desert animal, in the composition. It is crucial, however, to maintain a respectful distance, using zoom lenses to capture close-up shots of the flowers or birds without disrupting the natural behavior of the desert's inhabitants or harming the plant itself.

For a deeper understanding of these desert giants and their environment, Saguaro National Park offers ranger-led tours that delve into the fascinating world of desert ecology. These tours provide insights not only into the life of the saguaro cactus but also into the various survival strategies employed by flora and fauna in this extreme environment. The guides, often park rangers with extensive knowledge of the region, explain the interactions within desert ecosystems, including the relationships between plants and pollinators and the adaptations of desert wildlife. These educational tours are invaluable for any visitor eager to learn about the complexities of desert ecosystems and the importance of conservation efforts in preserving these fragile habitats.

Hiking through Saguaro National Park brings you face-to-face with the challenges of navigating a desert terrain. Safety is paramount when temperatures can soar to extreme highs and shade is scarce. Preparation begins with adequate hydration—carrying at least one gallon of water per person per day is recommended, along with electrolyte replacements to prevent dehydration. Dressing appropriately is also critical; lightweight, light-colored clothing, broad-brimmed hats, and UV protection sunglasses help manage sun exposure. Always check the weather before heading out, as summer monsoons can bring sudden flash floods, and have a map or GPS device at hand since trails can be less distinct in desert landscapes. Letting someone know your planned route and expected return time is a wise precaution. By adhering to these safety guidelines, your journey through Saguaro National Park becomes an exploration of its stunning landscapes and towering cacti and an exercise in responsible and safe desert hiking, ensuring that the beauty of the desert can be enjoyed without undue risk.

4.6 White Sands National Park: Sledding on Gypsum Dunes

At White Sands National Park, the undulating dunes of glistening gypsum offer a surreal playground unlike any other on Earth. Here, sledding transcends typical winter pastimes, presenting a year-round opportunity for adventure against a backdrop of stark, ethereal beauty. For both the young and the young at heart, sledding down these extraordinary white dunes provides exhilaration and a unique way to connect with the natural world. Selecting the correct type of sled is essential to partake in this joyous activity. Traditional snow sleds often do not work well on the fine gypsum sand. Instead, opt for waxed, plastic saucers or sleds designed explicitly for sand; these allow for a smoother ride and faster speeds. Before your descent, check the slope for any obstacles, such as plants or rocks, and choose a hill that ends with a gentle, flat area to ensure a safe stop. Applying wax to the bottom of your sled can enhance the slickness and speed, providing a more thrilling glide down the dunes.

The creation of these magnificent white dunes began with the mineral gypsum, a soft sulfate material rarely found in the form of sand due to its solubility in water. However, the unique conditions in the Tularosa Basin, where White Sands is located, allow this natural wonder to exist. The basin is enclosed, preventing the loss of minerals through water flow to the ocean, and with the evaporation of the shallow waters of the ancient Lake Lucero, gypsum is left behind, crystallizing into selenite. Over time, the relentless winds fracture the selenite crystals into fine, white sand, which the winds sculpted into the dune field that spreads across 275 square miles. This dynamic landscape shaped by the natural elements makes the dunes a perpetually changing environment, where patterns and shapes shift and evolve, driven by the prevailing winds.

Figure 20 White Sands National Park

Capturing the stunning landscapes of White Sands National Park offers a delightful challenge to any photographer. The best times for photography are during the golden hours of early morning and late afternoon when the sun is low in the sky. This lighting accentuates the ripples and contours of the dunes, casting shadows that highlight the texture of the sand and creating a dramatic contrast with the bright whiteness of the gypsum. The park's open vistas and minimal vegetation allow for unobstructed shots of the dune field, with the San Andres Mountains providing a majestic backdrop. A wide-angle lens is beneficial for capturing the grandeur of the landscape, allowing for a vast expanse of dunes to be included in the frame. Additionally, considering the high reflectivity of the gypsum sand, adjusting the exposure settings on your camera can prevent the white sand from appearing overexposed, ensuring the subtle details of the sand are preserved in your photographs.

Environmental responsibility is paramount in preserving the pristine condition of White Sands National Park. The dunes are a place of beauty and recreation and an ecosystem supporting a variety of life adapted to the harsh conditions of the gypsum dunes. As visitors enjoy the unique experience of sledding or exploring, minimizing the impact on this delicate environment is vital. Staying on designated trails and sledding areas helps protect the native plants and animals that rely on undisturbed dunes for survival. Additionally, packing out all trash, including broken sled pieces, ensures that the sands remain clean and the wildlife unharmed. The park operates under a "pack it in, pack it out" policy, which is crucial for maintaining the ecological balance and scenic beauty of White Sands.

As the sun sets on the white horizon, casting a soft pink glow over the dunes, the experiences at White Sands National Park linger in the memory, a vivid reminder of nature's capacity to surprise and delight. The park's blend of adventure, science, and conservation provides a profound connection to the natural world, encouraging a deeper appreciation for the delicate interplay of elements that shape our planet. The gypsum dunes of White Sands stand as a testament to the beauty and mystery of Earth's landscapes, offering endless inspiration and a serene escape into the vast, open wilderness.

As we conclude our exploration of the desert landscapes, we carry forward a sense of wonder and respect for these harsh yet profoundly beautiful environments. Each park and preserve offers a unique window into the resilience and beauty of nature's designs, teaching us valuable lessons about adaptation, conservation, and the enduring allure of the natural world. As we turn the pages to the next chapter, we continue our journey through America's diverse and splendid national parks, each chapter unfolding new landscapes, stories, and opportunities for discovery.

Make a Difference with Your Review

Unlock the Power of Generosity

"The parks do not belong to one state or to one section. The Yosemite, the Yellowstone, the Grand Canyon are national properties in which every citizen has a vested interest; they belong as much to the man of Massachusetts, of Michigan, of Florida, as they do to the people of California, of Wyoming, and of Arizona." – Stephen T. Mather, first director of the National Park Service.

To make that happen, I have a question for you...

Would you help someone you have never met, even if you never got credit for it?

Who is this person, you ask? They are like you. Or, at least, like you used to be. Less experienced, wanting to make a difference, and needing help, but unsure where to look.

Our mission is to make national parks accessible to everyone. Everything I do stems from that mission, and the only way for me to accomplish that mission is by reaching... everyone.

This is where you come in. Most people judge a book by its cover (and its reviews). So here's my ask on behalf of a struggling explorer you've never met:

Please help that explorer by leaving this book a review.

Your gift costs no money and less than 60 seconds to make real, but it can change a fellow explorer's life forever. Your review could help...

- ...one more small business provide for their community.
- ...one more entrepreneur support their family.
- ...one more employee get meaningful work.
- ...one more client transform their life.
- ...one more dream come true.

To get that 'feel good' feeling and help this person for real, all you have to do is leave a review, and it takes less than 60 seconds.

Simply scan the QR code below to leave your review:

If you feel good about helping a faceless explorer, you are my kind of person. Welcome to the club. You are one of us.

I am even more excited to help you explore our national parks than you imagine. You will love the lessons I share in the coming chapters.

Thank you from the bottom of my heart. Now, back to our regularly scheduled programming.

Your biggest fan, W.R. Hoover

PS - Fun fact: If you provide something of value to another person, it makes you more valuable to them. If you want goodwill straight from another explorer - and believe this book will help them - send it their way.

Chapter 5: Trip Planning and Logistics

Imagine planning your visit to a national park at a time when the trails are less trodden, the air is crisp with the just-right touch of seasonal charm, and the landmarks stand unobscured by crowds. This chapter is your compass to navigating the nuances of park visitation, ensuring that your journey into nature's embrace is as serene and enriching as possible.

5.1 Navigating Peak Seasons: Best Times to Visit

Crowd Avoidance Strategies: Identifying less crowded times to visit popular parks.

The allure of national parks often means sharing their beauty with others. Yet, with some strategic planning, you can find tranquility and peace even in the most visited parks. Timing your visit during the shoulder seasons—late spring or early autumn—can significantly reduce the number of encounters on the trails and at scenic viewpoints. For instance, visiting Yosemite in late September allows you to enjoy the fading gold of the sunlit meadows with fewer companions than you would in mid-summer. Similarly, the weeks following Labor Day, when schools are back in session, offer a quieter experience in most parks. Utilizing weekdays rather than weekends can also transform your visit, offering quieter trails and more intimate connections with the park's natural wonders. Remember that some parks, like those in the desert regions, may have peak seasons that differ due to extreme summer temperatures, making cooler months more crowded.

Seasonal Weather Patterns: How weather varies across seasons in different parks and how it affects visitation.

Weather plays a pivotal role in shaping your national park experience, influencing not only the landscape but also accessibility and comfort. Understanding the seasonal weather patterns of your chosen destination is crucial. For example, the Great Smoky Mountains National Park offers a lush, verdant landscape in summer. Still, if you prefer solitude and mesmerizing frosty mornings, winter might be your ideal season to visit.

Conversely, the arid landscapes of Death Valley National Park are best visited in the cooler months from November to March, when the brutal summer heat subsides and the lower temperatures make exploration enjoyable. Always check the historical weather conditions and prepare accordingly, as weather can impact park services, road accessibility, and trail conditions. This knowledge will empower you to make the most of your park visit.

Event Timing: Key events and natural phenomena that can determine the best time to visit.

Aligning your visit with specific natural events or annual festivals can enhance your experience. Many parks offer unique natural displays or cultural events depending on the time of year. For instance, if you wish to witness the synchronous fireflies—a natural phenomenon—you should plan to visit the Great Smoky Mountains National Park in early June. Alternatively, if floral blooms captivate you, aim for a spring visit to Shenandoah National Park to see the wildflowers in full display. Additionally, consider local festivals and events that can offer deeper insights into the region's culture and history. These events are often listed on the park's official website and can provide a memorable highlight to your visit.

Booking Advance Permits: Early planning for permits during peak seasons is essential.

You may need to secure permits for specific activities and areas within national parks, especially during peak visiting times. Early application is crucial, whether backcountry camping, hiking in sensitive ecosystems, or attending a popular event. Parks like Yosemite and Zion require advance permits for activities like the Half Dome hike or overnight stays in the wilderness. Due to high demand, these permits are often issued months in advance via a lottery system. Planning ensures you adhere to park regulations and secures your spot, allowing you to fully immerse yourself in the experience without the worry of logistical hiccups. Always check the specific park's website for details on how and when to apply for permits. This proactive approach is essential for a smooth and fulfilling visit, allowing you to focus on the beauty and adventure that awaits in America's stunning national parks.

Exploring these majestic lands requires thoughtful planning to align with your preferences, the park's seasonal characteristics, and the logistical demands of popular destinations. Considering these factors, your visit can transform from a simple getaway into a profound experience of nature's unspoiled splendors.

5.2 Budget-Friendly National Park Vacations: Tips and Tricks

Exploring the majestic landscapes of America's national parks does not have to strain your wallet. With a bit of savvy planning and some insider knowledge, you can enjoy the full splendor of these natural treasures while maintaining a budget that keeps your finances in check. From sleeping under the stars to enjoying the wealth of free educational programs, let us uncover how you can maximize your national park experience without breaking the bank.

Cost-Saving Accommodation Options: Camping guide, RV stays, and affordable lodging.

Accommodations often constitute one of the most significant travel expenses, but national parks offer several budget-friendly options. Camping is typically the most economical choice, with many parks providing campgrounds that range from primitive backcountry sites to well-equipped grounds with amenities like restrooms and running water. If you are not up for a tent experience, consider renting an RV, which combines transportation and lodging costs and provides a comfortable place to sleep and cook. Many parks have designated RV sites with hook-ups for electricity and water. For a more traditional stay, investigate lodges or cabins within the park, which often offer a more affordable rate than comparable hotels outside the park. Additionally, some parks are near national forest land or other public lands, where dispersed camping is allowed for free or a nominal fee. Always make reservations as far in advance as possible, especially if you plan to visit during peak seasons.

Park Passes and Fee-Free Days: Leveraging annual passes and fee-free days for savings.

To maximize your savings while exploring multiple parks within a year, consider investing in an America the Beautiful Pass. This annual pass covers entrance fees at over 2,000 federal recreation sites, including all national parks that charge an entrance fee. The pass is especially valuable for families or groups, as it covers entry for drivers and passengers in a personal vehicle. Additionally, keep an eye out for fee-free days. Several times a year, all national parks offer free admission to everyone. These dates often coincide with significant public holidays or events like National Public Lands Day or the National Park Service Anniversary. Planning your trips around these dates can save on entrance fees and allow you to explore the parks' riches without spending a penny on admission.

Economical Eating: Packing and preparing meals to save on food costs.

Dining out during park visits can quickly add up, but with some preparation, you can eat well without the excessive cost. Before your trip, plan your meals and pack ingredients. Utilize coolers for perishables, and bring a portable stove or grill if you are camping. Many parks allow you to use picnic areas to cook and enjoy your meals amidst scenic views. Consider preparing food at your campsite or lodging and packing picnic lunches for your hikes. Not only will this save money, but it will also allow you to eat healthily and on your schedule. Additionally, always carry plenty of snacks and water. Buying these items in a park, especially at remote locations, can be expensive due to limited supply.

Free and Low-Cost Activities: Highlighting free ranger-led programs and self-guided activities.

One of the great rewards of national parks is the abundance of free and low-cost activities available. Most parks offer free ranger-led programs, including guided hikes, wildlife talks, and evening campfire programs. These programs provide valuable insights into the park's ecology, geology, and history from knowledgeable park staff. Many parks also have self-guided trails with interpretive signs that teach you about the area at your own pace. Visitor centers often provide free maps and educational exhibits and are staffed by rangers eager to share tips and information about the park. For families, do not forget to ask about the Junior Ranger Program, which offers free activity books and the opportunity for kids to earn a badge by learning about the park.

Exploring national parks should be about making lasting memories, not overspending. With these cost-effective strategies, you ensure that your visit is as affordable as it is memorable, allowing you to fully immerse yourself in the natural beauty and grandeur of America's greatest natural assets. Whether setting up a tent under the stars, learning from a park ranger, or enjoying a homemade meal against the backdrop of mountains and meadows, these tips help you enjoy a rich park experience that keeps your budget intact.

5.3 Packing for the Parks: Essentials for Every Climate

When preparing for a trip to a national park, your packing list can be as diverse as the landscapes you plan to explore. Each environment demands specific gear to navigate its unique challenges, from the arid deserts to the misty mountains. A well-thought-out packing strategy ensures comfort and safety, allowing you to enjoy the natural beauty around you without the distraction of being unprepared.

Layering for Variable Weather: Advice on clothing layers to manage changing conditions.

The key to staying comfortable in any park climate lies in mastering the art of layering. Start with a moisture-wicking base layer that keeps your skin dry by drawing sweat away, which is essential in hot and cold conditions. For your middle layer, opt for something insulating like fleece or wool, which traps heat efficiently. This layer can be adjusted based on the temperature and your activity level, making it versatile for varying conditions throughout the day. The outermost layer should be waterproof and windproof, shielding you from rain, snow, or wind. This system keeps you prepared for sudden weather changes and allows you to add or remove layers as needed throughout the day. For instance, morning hikes in higher elevations might start chilly but warm up quickly as the sun rises and your exertion increases. You can adapt seamlessly without returning to base camp by dressing in layers.

Must-Have Gear: Essential items for safety and comfort in various park environments.

Beyond clothing, several must-have items should be in your backpack regardless of the park or climate. Sturdy hiking boots offer the necessary support and protection over rough trails. A high-quality, broad-spectrum sunscreen protects your skin from UV rays at all altitudes. A first-aid kit for minor injuries is crucial, especially in remote areas of large parks. Water purification methods, such as a filter or purification tablets, ensure you can hydrate safely wherever your hikes take you. Lastly, a reliable multi-tool can prove indispensable in unexpected situations, from repairing gear to preparing a meal. Each of these items plays a critical role in your comfort and safety, making them non-negotiable essentials on your packing list.

Lightweight Packing Tips: Strategies for minimizing backpack weight while ensuring preparedness.

Efficient packing is critical, especially for extended treks where every ounce matters. Start by selecting a lightweight, durable backpack with good support and multiple compartments for easy organization. Invest in travel-sized containers for toiletries and opt for multi-use items wherever possible, like soap that can be used for your body, dishes, and clothes. When it comes to food, choose dehydrated or freeze-dried meals that are light and just require water. Packing items that serve more than one purpose, such as a scarf that can be used for warmth, sun protection, or as a makeshift towel, also helps reduce your load. Each item in your pack should earn its place based on necessity and frequency of use. You enhance your mobility and endurance on the trail by prioritizing and streamlining what you carry.

Specialized Equipment: Recommendations for activity-specific gear such as binoculars for bird watching or crampons for glacier hiking.

Specific activities in national parks call for specialized equipment that can enhance your experience significantly. For bird watchers, a good pair of lightweight, waterproof binoculars can bring distant wildlife into clear view, transforming a simple hike into an engaging wildlife observation excursion. Likewise, if your park adventure includes traversing icy terrain, crampons can provide the necessary grip to navigate slippery surfaces safely, preventing falls and injuries. Similarly, a sturdy yet lightweight trekking pole can offer valuable stability and support across diverse terrains, from steep mountain paths to uneven desert trails. Tailoring your gear to the specific activities you plan to undertake increases your safety and enjoyment, allowing you to engage with the environment and its offerings fully. By considering these specialized tools as integral to your packing list, you ensure that you are prepared for the general demands of park exploration and equipped to dive deep into the specific experiences that await in each unique landscape.

Packing for a national park visit thus becomes a carefully balanced act of preparing for safety, comfort, and specific environmental conditions. With the right gear and a thoughtful approach to what you carry, you set the stage for a seamless and memorable outdoor experience. You will be fully immersed in the natural wonders around you, ready to meet the adventures that lie ahead.

5.4 Finding the Perfect Place to Stay: Lodging Inside and Near the Parks

Planning your escapade to the national parks, where you decide to rest each night, is integral in shaping your overall experience. The options for accommodations vary widely, from the rustic charm of park lodges nestled in scenic locales to the practical comforts of nearby hotels and unique alternatives like cabins and hostels. Each type of lodging offers distinct advantages and experiences, catering to different tastes and needs. Park lodges, often within the park boundaries, provide unparalleled access to trails and landmarks. These lodges range from luxurious historic hotels with fine dining options to modest cabins with basic amenities, allowing you to choose according to your comfort and budget preferences. On the other hand, staying in hotels outside the park can be a cost-effective choice, often providing modern amenities such as Wi-Fi and swimming pools and the flexibility to explore the surrounding community's attractions.

For the adventurous spirit, backcountry camping presents a way to connect with the natural environment deeply. Designated backcountry campsites offer a more secluded and immersive experience, allowing you to wake up surrounded by pristine landscapes, often unreachable by day-trippers. This option requires more preparation and adherence to strict park regulations to ensure safety and minimize environmental impact. Still, the reward is a profound sense of solitude and communion with nature. It is crucial to secure permits early, as these spots are limited and in high demand, especially in well-known parks like Yellowstone and Yosemite.

Booking Strategies: Tips for securing accommodations, especially in high-demand areas.

Securing a place to stay in or near popular national parks, especially during peak visitation seasons, demands strategy and early action. Begin by defining your preferred base—inside the park for closer access to nature or outside for more amenities and value. For lodgings inside the park, it is advisable to book as soon as reservations open, which can be up to a year in advance for some of the more popular destinations. Many parks use a reservation system that releases blocks of bookings periodically throughout the year, so understanding this schedule can increase your chances of securing a spot. Websites and customer service lines can be overwhelmed with traffic when new reservations are released, so persistence and patience are key. Consider alternative dates and be flexible with your plans, as you might find availability just outside your ideal travel window.

For those looking outside the park boundaries, a wealth of options typically exists, from chain hotels and quaint bed-and-breakfasts to unique local rentals found on platforms like Airbnb. Booking sites often offer the ability to set alerts for price drops or new availability, which can help you snag a good deal even in high-demand locales. Another effective strategy is to look for accommodations in lesser-known areas slightly further from the park entrances but still convenient for daily excursions. These often-overlooked locales can offer better rates and availability and a more authentic local experience.

Alternative Accommodations: Exploring lesser-known options like cabins, hostels, and B&Bs.

Venturing beyond traditional hotels and campgrounds can lead you to charming and economical lodging options that enhance your visit with local flavor and coziness. Cabins, often available inside and outside the parks, provide a delightful balance between the rustic feel of camping and the comforts of home, with options ranging from basic no-frills to fully equipped luxury. Hostels are an excellent choice for solo travelers or those on a tight budget, offering low-cost lodging and a social atmosphere that can be great for meeting fellow travelers. Many hostels also offer private rooms and dormitory-style accommodations, catering to those who desire privacy and affordability.

Bed and breakfasts (B&Bs) are perfect for those seeking a homely touch. They often include homemade meals and personalized service. B&Bs, usually run by locals, offer invaluable insights into the area and tailored recommendations for exploring the region. This type of accommodation can often be found in scenic locations that provide a unique perspective on the area's natural beauty, away from the more commercialized tourist spots.

Stay Close, Explore More: Benefits of staying within or near the park boundaries for timely access and late exploration.

Choosing lodging close to or within the park boundaries can profoundly impact your experience, allowing you to maximize your time in nature. One significant advantage is the ability to beat the crowds to popular spots, enjoying peaceful mornings and evenings when wildlife is most active and other visitors are few. Early risers experience the magic of sunrise illuminating the landscapes, and staying late lets you witness the sunset colors transforming the scenery. Proximity also offers the flexibility to return to your lodging for midday breaks or unexpected needs, making your visit more relaxed and accommodating to personal rhythms.

Moreover, staying close keeps you attuned to the park's nocturnal life and celestial shows. Many parks offer night programs or have dark sky status for stargazing, experiences that are significantly enhanced without the worry of long drives back to distant accommodations. The convenience of nearby lodging allows for deeper immersion and a more satisfying connection to the natural wonders you came to experience, wrapping each day up with the tranquil sense of being just steps away from the wild.

5.5 Accessibility in the Parks: Ensuring an Inclusive Experience

The beauty of nature should be available to everyone, and ensuring accessibility in our national parks is a priority that helps all visitors, regardless of physical ability, enjoy the splendors of the great outdoors. Many parks across the country have made significant strides in providing accessible trails, viewpoints, and facilities that cater to visitors with disabilities, allowing everyone to experience the parks' natural wonders firsthand. These accessible features are thoughtfully designed to ensure safety and ease of access while preserving the natural environment. For example, paved or firm gravel trails with gentle grades and resting areas offer those with mobility challenges or families using strollers the chance to explore without the stress of navigating rough terrain. Additionally, many parks now feature accessible viewpoints that provide breathtaking views of landscapes, ensuring that all visitors can capture the beauty of iconic park vistas. Restrooms, picnic areas, and campsites are also being adapted to meet accessibility standards, featuring wider doors, appropriate heights for counters, and accessible pathways connecting these amenities.

Planning a visit to a national park with accessibility needs in mind requires some research and preparation, but the rewards are immense. The National Park Service (NPS) provides detailed accessibility information on its website for each park, outlining the accessible services, features, and activities available. Many parks offer free, downloadable accessibility guides with maps and descriptions of trails, attractions, and services specifically geared toward visitors with disabilities. It is also helpful to contact the park directly before your visit to inquire about any specific needs you might have. Park staff can often provide up-to-date information about accessible facilities and programs. They also may offer recommendations based on your interests and abilities. Additionally, many parks provide loaner wheelchairs on a first-come, first-served basis, and some even offer specialized equipment like beach wheelchairs that can navigate sandy areas, ensuring you can enjoy a wide range of park environments.

Including adaptive programs and tours is another exciting development making national parks more accessible. These programs are designed to accommodate visitors of all abilities. They can include tactile tours for visitors who are blind or have low vision, sign language interpretation for events and programs, and adaptive sports programs that allow for participation in activities such as kayaking, cycling, and hiking. For instance, several parks now collaborate with organizations that specialize in adaptive sports to offer guided hikes using specialized wheelchairs that can manage rugged terrain, allowing participants to explore areas of the park they might not have thought possible. These programs provide practical solutions and enhance the park experience, fostering a sense of inclusion and community among all visitors.

Visitor centers are pivotal in enhancing the national park experience for all guests, serving as hubs of information and resources. These centers have accessible parking, entryways, and interior spaces to ensure all visitors, including those with disabilities, can use the facilities comfortably. Inside, you will find exhibits and displays designed to be inclusive, with features like audio descriptions, tactile models, and interactive elements at accessible heights. Staff at visitor centers are also an excellent resource for personalized information and assistance, helping you plan your day in the park to maximize your experience based on your specific needs. They can provide the latest information on accessible trails, programs, and any temporary accessibility changes due to weather or construction. Utilizing these services ensures your visit is enjoyable and full of the rich educational opportunities national parks offer.

Ensuring accessibility in national parks is about creating opportunities for all visitors to experience nature's profound beauty and transformative power. As these efforts evolve, they reflect a broader commitment to inclusivity and accessibility in our public spaces, inviting everyone to explore, learn, and be inspired by the natural world. Whether through the thoughtful design of facilities, the careful planning of accessible programs, or the dedicated service provided by national park staff, these initiatives ensure that our parks remain welcoming and accessible to everyone today and into the future.

5.6 The Digital Nomad's Guide to National Parks: Connectivity Spots

In an era where work and lifestyle flexibility has become increasingly prevalent, national parks are adapting to accommodate the needs of digital nomads seeking the grandeur of nature without disconnecting completely from their professional responsibilities. Knowing where and how you can access the internet in these vast natural spaces is crucial as you blend productivity with exploration. Several parks now offer Wi-Fi hotspots, primarily located around visitor centers, lodges, and some campgrounds. These connectivity hubs allow you to check emails, attend virtual meetings, or manage urgent tasks amidst your adventures. For example, areas around Yosemite Valley Lodge and the Ahwahnee Hotel provide Wi-Fi for guests and visitors, making it feasible to connect with the outside world, even from the heart of Yosemite National Park. Similarly, Yellowstone has connectivity options in developed areas like Old Faithful and Mammoth Hot Springs. While Wi-Fi in these locations may not always match urban broadband speeds, it is sufficient for most basic online tasks.

Balancing work with the immersive experience of park exploration requires a well-thought-out plan. Start your day early by tackling the most demanding work tasks during the quiet morning hours, leaving your afternoons and evenings free for hiking, photography, and wildlife watching. This aligns with most individuals' productive peaks and helps you avoid the midday sun in many parks, making your outdoor activities more pleasant. Additionally, setting clear boundaries and expectations with your colleagues and clients about your availability can reduce stress and allow you to enjoy your natural surroundings more fully. Informing them of your park itinerary and the times you plan to be offline helps manage project timelines and ensures that your work commitments are met without compromising your park experience.

For the digital nomad, packing the right tech gear is as essential as a water bottle or hiking boots. Your mobile office must be lightweight, functional, and adaptable to various outdoor conditions. A durable, water-resistant laptop or tablet with a long battery life and a portable power bank are necessary to recharge devices when electrical outlets are scarce. Solar chargers also offer a sustainable option to power your gadgets, leveraging the abundant sunshine in many parks. Do not forget a reliable mobile hotspot device, which can provide an internet connection through cellular networks when Wi-Fi is unavailable. Ensure your data plan is robust enough to manage your work needs, primarily if you rely on cloud services or need to upload and download large files. A protective, shock-absorbent case for your electronics and a lightweight, compact travel desk can also enhance your mobile workspace, providing stability and security for your devices in rugged outdoor settings.

While staying connected has advantages, the opportunity for a digital detox is a significant draw of national park visits. Many areas within these parks are free from the reach of Wi-Fi and cell service, offering a perfect setting to unplug and immerse yourself in the natural environment. These tech-free zones encourage you to fully engage with the serene landscapes, listen to the subtle sounds of nature, and reconnect with your thoughts without the constant interruption of digital notifications. Embrace these moments by keeping electronic devices turned off or in airplane mode, allowing yourself to be present and genuinely attentive to the wonders around you. Whether it is the quiet majesty of towering trees, the soothing sounds of a babbling brook, or the thrill of spotting wildlife in their natural habitat, the sensory richness of these experiences can be profoundly revitalizing and offer a much-needed contrast to the screen-focused lifestyle.

As this chapter closes, remember that blending the digital nomad lifestyle with the explorative spirit of a national park visitor offers the best of both worlds. By leveraging spots with connectivity, balancing your work obligations with the call of the wild, equipping yourself with the right technology, and embracing opportunities to disconnect, you create a fulfilling and productive experience that enriches your professional and personal life. As we transition from the logistics of travel planning to the exciting adventures that await in the parks, let these insights guide you in crafting an impactful and inspiring journey where work meets play in the most scenic of offices.

Chapter 6: Safety, Conservation, and Etiquette

As you step into our national parks' vast, breathing landscapes, you are not just a visitor but a participant in a delicate ecological ballet. Each creature, from the towering elk to the elusive mountain lion, plays a role in a delicately balanced ecosystem. Here, the whisper of wings or the rustle of underbrush holds stories of survival and interdependence. This chapter is dedicated to fostering harmonious encounters with wildlife, ensuring your safety and the well-being of the natural inhabitants. By understanding the appropriate ways to interact with the wildlife you come to admire, you contribute to the preservation of these magnificent creatures and their homes for generations to come.

6.1 Wildlife Encounters: Safety and Respect

Safe Wildlife Viewing

Observing wildlife in their natural habitat is a privilege that carries a responsibility to act as a respectful spectator. Maintaining a safe distance is not just a rule; it is a crucial step for your safety and the prevention of disturbing animals. Each species may require different viewing distances, often provided by park regulations. For example, keeping at least one hundred yards away from predators like bears and wolves and twenty-five yards from other wildlife such as deer and elk is a standard guideline. Use binoculars or a telephoto lens to experience close-up views without encroaching on the animals' space. This respectful observation ensures that wildlife continues their natural behavior undisturbed by human interference, allowing for a genuine experience of nature's raw beauty.

Feeding Wildlife

Though often well-intentioned, the act of feeding wildlife undermines the natural order of the park's ecosystems. Human food can harm animals, leading to nutritional deficiencies and health problems. Moreover, animals accustomed to human food may alter their natural behaviors, becoming aggressive or dependent on human-provided resources. This dependency can also increase their mortality risk from vehicle strikes or predation as they venture closer to human habitats. It is vital to adhere to park rules prohibiting feeding wildlife, ensuring these creatures remain wild and free, and sourcing their sustenance from their natural environment.

Encounter Protocols

Unexpected wildlife encounters can be startling. Knowing how to react can protect both you and the animal. If you find yourself close to a large animal, do not run; this could trigger a predatory response. Instead, stay calm, slowly back away, and avoid direct eye contact, which can be perceived as challenging. Speak softly to inform the animal of your presence since many incidents occur when animals are surprised or feel threatened. In the case of a bear encounter, use bear spray as a deterrent if the bear shows aggressive behavior. Being prepared and knowledgeable about these encounter protocols can significantly increase the safety of both visitors and wildlife.

Photography Ethics

Capturing wildlife images is a way to preserve your memories and share the beauty of nature with others. However, it is crucial to do so ethically. Wildlife photographers should adhere to guidelines prioritizing the animal's well-being over the shot. This includes using appropriate zoom lenses to maintain a safe distance, avoiding actions that could provoke or stress the animal, and being patient rather than trying to alter the scene for a better picture. The subject's welfare should always come first, ensuring that our practices as observers do not harm wildlife's natural behaviors and habitats.

Photographing wildlife responsibly also extends to sharing images on social media. Consider the potential impacts of posting locations of sensitive or endangered species, as these can lead to disturbances if areas become overrun by visitors. Practicing and promoting ethical photography contributes to conservation efforts and helps foster a community of respectful wildlife enthusiasts.

In this chapter, while exploring the intertwined themes of safety, respect, and ethical interaction with wildlife, you are equipped with guidelines and the principles behind them. As you move through the diverse ecosystems of our national parks, your informed and considerate actions ensure that these sanctuaries remain vibrant and vital. Here, in the quiet moments spent under the vast sky or in the thrill of spotting a rare bird, you find that ardent appreciation of nature comes from observing its untamed, uninterrupted majesty. This reverence for the wild, carried in the hearts of all who wander these paths, preserves our national parks' spirit and splendor.

6.2 Leave No Trace: Principles for Park Visitors

The serene call of the wild that draws millions to our national parks yearly is the same siren song that beckons us to protect these precious resources. Embracing the Leave No Trace principles provides a framework for conservation that ensures our park visits contribute positively to the ecosystem. These principles, tailored specifically for the vast and diverse environments of national parks, serve as a guide to minimize our impact and preserve the natural beauty for future explorers.

The first principle, Plan and Prepare, is crucial in minimizing impact. This involves understanding the specific regulations and unique concerns of the park you visit. Each park may have different rules regarding trail use, campfires, and wildlife interactions. By planning, you ensure that your visit complies with park regulations and aligns with conservation efforts. For instance, knowing the permitted areas for camping and the trails suited to your experience level can prevent unintended damage to undeveloped park areas and ensure your safety.

The principle of Travel and Camp on Durable Surfaces is essential in protecting the park's integrity. Stick to established trails and campsites. Veering off the designated paths can lead to soil erosion and the destruction of young vegetation, which can take years to recover. The sheer volume of visitors in popular parks can magnify this impact significantly. When camping, use clearly defined sites so that further vegetation damage will not occur. These practices ensure that the parks' trails and sites remain pristine and inviting for all who follow.

The third principle, Dispose of Waste Properly, is a cornerstone of park stewardship. This means packing out trash and food scraps, which can otherwise attract wildlife and lead to unhealthy dependencies on human food. Moreover, human waste should be handled appropriately. In areas without restroom facilities, bury human waste in a small hole 6 to 8 inches deep and at least two hundred feet from any water source, trail, or campsite. This practice prevents contamination of water sources and minimizes the likelihood of unpleasant encounters for other visitors.

Lastly, Leave What You Find encapsulates the essence of preserving our parks' natural and cultural treasures. Avoid moving rocks, picking plants or flowers, and disturbing historical artifacts. Each park ecosystem component, whether a fallen leaf or a historic relic, plays a role in the park's story. By leaving these items as you find them, you preserve the park's legacy and ensure that others enjoy the same sense of discovery and wonder.

Minimizing Campfire Impacts

The glow of a campfire can be one of the most enchanting experiences in a national park, yet how we manage this simple pleasure can have lasting effects on the environment. To minimize your impact, use established fire rings and keep fires small. This practice concentrates the impact on areas already affected and reduces the likelihood of the fire spreading. Always check fire regulations before you light a fire, as restrictions are often in place depending on the season and conditions, which can change rapidly. If campfires are not allowed, or if you wish to leave no trace, consider using a portable stove for cooking and an LED lantern for lighting. When it is time to put the fire out, water it until you can handle the ashes with your bare hands to ensure it is completely extinguished. This meticulous approach to managing campfires helps protect the park's resources and reduces the risk of wildfires, which can devastate thousands of acres.

Trail Etiquette

Sharing the trails respectfully with other visitors and wildlife ensures a positive experience for everyone and helps maintain the natural habitat. Keep to the right side of the trail and let others pass on the left. When hiking in groups, avoid spreading out and creating new trails. If you encounter horses or pack animals, step off the trail on the downhill side to let them pass, as this is less threatening to the animals. In terms of noise, keep voices low and avoid playing loud music; the natural sounds of the park are part of its allure. This consideration for others enhances the experience while preserving the tranquil atmosphere many seek in nature.

Waste Management

Effective waste management is crucial in preserving the park environment. Always carry a trash bag and pack out all garbage, including food wrappers, fruit peels, and even biodegradable items, as these can take much longer to decompose in a natural setting than you might expect. Be meticulous in cleaning up after meals at camp and checking the ground for crumbs or spills, which can attract wildlife. For feminine hygiene products, toilet paper, and other personal waste, use resealable bags to pack them out. Many parks also provide bear-proof trash receptacles at trailheads and developed areas; use these facilities to dispose of your garbage correctly, thus reducing the chance of attracting wildlife and contributing to their habituation to human presence.

By adhering to these principles and practices, you enjoy the immense beauty and serenity of our national parks and take active steps in preserving these treasures. Each action, from planning your trip to the way you manage waste, intertwines with a collective effort to ensure that these natural sanctuaries continue to inspire and awe all who visit, now and in the future.

6.3 Fire Safety in National Parks: A Critical Guide

In the embrace of nature's vast expanses, the crackle of a campfire often brings a sense of comfort and conviviality. However, the management of these fires within national parks must be approached with a vigilant understanding of regulations and fire's raw power. Adhering to fire bans and restrictions is not merely a suggestion—it is an essential part of your responsibility as a visitor. Fire regulations are established based on current weather conditions, the amount of moisture in the vegetation, and other factors that affect fire danger. These rules are vital for the safety of all park visitors and the preservation of natural resources. Ignoring these regulations can have severe consequences, leading to uncontrolled wildfires that devastate ecosystems and endanger lives. Always check the latest fire conditions at park entrances or visitor centers and respect all fire bans and restrictions. In areas where fires are permitted, it is crucial to use designated fire rings and never leave a fire unattended.

Creating a safe campfire, when allowed, starts with selecting the correct location. Always use existing fire rings to reduce the impact on the surrounding area. Clear all flammable materials away from the fire pit, including dry leaves and twigs, to prevent the accidental spreading of the fire. Keep fires small to minimize the chances of embers escaping, and have water or a shovel nearby to extinguish any stray sparks quickly. When it is time to retire for the night or when you leave the campsite, extinguishing your campfire entirely is a critical step that must never be overlooked. Douse the fire with water, stir the ashes with a stick or shovel, and apply more water. Repeat this process until the ashes are cool to the touch. Ensuring no smoldering embers remain is the only way to prevent potentially devastating wildfires.

Wildfire prevention is a responsibility shared by all who enjoy the parks' natural beauty. Beyond managing campfires, there are several practices you can adopt to help prevent wildfires. For instance, be cautious when parking vehicles over dry grasses, as the hot undercarriage can ignite the vegetation. If you smoke, always dispose of cigarette butts in designated containers—never toss them on the ground. Stay on established trails to avoid trampling and potentially igniting dry vegetation when hiking. These mindful behaviors significantly prevent wildfires, preserving the landscape's integrity and the safety of its diverse habitats.

Knowing how to react can be lifesaving if you encounter a wildfire during your visit. First, remain calm and assess the situation. If the fire is small and you are confident in your ability to extinguish it, use water or dirt to smother it. However, if the fire has spread beyond immediate control, prioritize evacuation. Notify Park authorities as soon as possible by calling 911 or using emergency communication devices often found in remote areas of the park. Follow posted evacuation routes designed to lead you to safety efficiently. If specific routes are unavailable, move away from the fire, favoring routes that lead downhill as fires spread more rapidly uphill. Throughout your evacuation, stay aware of your surroundings, watching for changes in the direction of the fire due to wind shifts.

Navigating the challenges of fire safety in national parks with respect and preparedness ensures that these cherished environments and those who visit them remain safe. By understanding and implementing the guidelines for fire management and wildfire prevention, your actions contribute to a culture of conscientious park enjoyment and environmental stewardship. As you gather around the warmth of a responsibly maintained campfire, you celebrate the beauty of the flames and the collective effort to protect and preserve the natural wonders entrusted to our care.

6.4 Conserving Water in Desert Parks: Do's and Don'ts

Water, the most vital of resources, takes on an even more critical role within the arid expanses of desert parks. Here, every drop counts for the survival of the park's flora and fauna and visitors who traverse these stark, beautiful landscapes. Water conservation principles in such environments extend beyond simple preservation; they are essential strategies for sustaining the delicate balance of desert ecosystems. Understanding how to use water sparingly while ensuring you remain adequately hydrated requires thoughtful preparation and an appreciation for the surroundings you are enjoying.

When planning your visit to a desert park, consider the limited water sources and the impact your water usage could have on the area. In these environments, water is not just a visitor's necessity but a lifeline for the native plants and animals adapted to the harsh conditions. To minimize your impact, carry all the water you might need for the day's activities, as relying on park resources can deplete the reserves that wildlife depends on. This practice also avoids straining the park's infrastructure, which is often not designed to accommodate excessive water use by large numbers of tourists. Moreover, when camping, opt for dry or sponge bathing instead of showers, and collect water used for washing dishes or similar tasks to avoid introducing soaps and detergents into the soil, which can disrupt local water chemistry and harm plant life.

Hydration is a grave concern in the dry heat of desert parks, where dehydration can occur quickly and with little warning. To manage hydration effectively, drink plenty of water before you begin your day's activities. Carrying a reusable water bottle helps track how much you drink and reduces waste. Electrolyte replacements can also be vital, especially during prolonged exposure to elevated temperatures, as they help replenish salts lost through sweat. Planning your activities during cooler parts of the day, such as early morning or late afternoon, can reduce sweat loss, helping to conserve your body's moisture. Always have more water than you think you need; it is better to carry back extra water than ration in the heat.

The impact of human activity on local water sources can be profound in desert environments. The introduction of pollutants, whether through runoff from campsites or oils from vehicles, can contaminate water sources that animals depend on for survival. Additionally, visitors' physical presence near water sources can lead to soil compaction, which changes the natural runoff patterns and can cause erosion. Always use established rest areas to mitigate these impacts and avoid creating new paths to water sources. If you must cross a stream, do so at designated crossing points where the effect will be minimal. Keeping a respectful distance from springs and other natural water features helps preserve these critical resources for the wildlife that depend on them.

Desert camping demands an elevated level of water use ethics. One practical method is using portable water tanks and solar showers, which contain water runoff and can be packed out, leaving no trace of your visit. When disposing of greywater, used water is scattered on rocks or gravel rather than in vegetation or water sources, as this helps the water evaporate quickly and minimizes its impact on the environment. In areas where water is scarce, consider minimizing activities that require excessive water use, such as cooking meals that need water for preparation. Opt for pre-prepared meals or snacks, which can significantly reduce the water required during your stay.

Every visitor plays a role in the conservation of these stunning yet sensitive desert landscapes. By adopting practices that respect the natural limits and needs of the environment, you contribute to the ongoing vitality and resilience of the park's ecosystem. Each careful step, from planning your water needs to minimizing your impact, intertwines with the broader efforts to ensure that these desert realms continue to inspire and awe all who wander their paths.

6.5 Cultural Heritage Sites: Visiting with Respect

When exploring the enriched tapestries of our national parks, you often tread paths that weave through areas steeped in profound cultural significance. These sites, ranging from ancient cliff dwellings to sacred burial grounds, are not just historical artifacts; they are living spaces of spiritual and cultural importance to Indigenous and local communities. Understanding how to approach these treasures with the utmost respect ensures these sites retain their integrity and significance for those who hold them dear. Observing proper etiquette during your visits to such places involves more than following posted rules—it is about embracing an attitude of reverence and stewardship.

Respect for sacred and cultural sites manifests in several ways, starting with recognizing these spaces as more than tourist destinations. For many communities, these are places of worship, ceremonial grounds, and crucial parts of their cultural heritage. Behaving with respect means keeping voices down, refraining from climbing on or touching culturally sensitive structures, and following all guidelines outlined by park authorities. Often, specific paths are designated to keep visitors at a respectful distance that protects both the physical site and the privacy of those who come here to carry out traditional practices. Attending any orientations or guided tours offered by the park is also important, as these can provide essential insights into the appropriate conduct expected from visitors, which might not be immediately apparent.

Educating yourself about the cultural significance of the sites you plan to visit adds depth to your experience while fostering respect for the traditions and histories of the local communities. Before your visit, learn about the site's history and place in the Indigenous culture. Many national parks have resources available, including visitor center exhibits, official park websites, and books written by or about the Indigenous communities associated with the sites. This knowledge enriches your visit and transforms your perspective, allowing you to see the landmarks as living narratives rather than static relics. Understanding the stories and significance behind these cultural sites shifts your visit from mere observation to an informed, respectful engagement with the culture.

Photography at cultural heritage sites is a subject that requires sensitive consideration. While capturing images of stunning archaeological sites or sacred landscapes can be tempting, it is crucial to be mindful of photography rules specific to each location. Some areas may restrict photography to preserve the site's sacredness or the privacy of people practicing cultural rituals. Always look for signage about photography policies, or ask a park ranger if unsure. When photography is allowed, ensure that your actions do not disrupt the site's sanctity or the experience of others who are there to pay their respects. This means unobtrusively using your camera, avoiding areas marked as private, and never using flash on sensitive artifacts or ceremonial activities.

Supporting Indigenous communities associated with national parks goes beyond respectful visitation practices; it involves engaging with these communities in a manner that acknowledges their sovereignty and ongoing connection to the land. One way to support these communities is by purchasing authentic crafts and goods from local Indigenous artists and vendors, often available at visitor centers or nearby town markets. These transactions help sustain the local economy and allow artisans to continue their cultural traditions. Additionally, consider participating in cultural events or guided tours led by community members. These programs provide authentic insights into the area's cultural heritage and ensure that your financial contributions directly benefit the community. Always approach these experiences as opportunities to learn and show respect, remembering you can share in someone else's cultural expressions.

As you move through these sacred spaces with a mindful step and an open heart, your experiences at these cultural heritage sites become more than just visits; they are opportunities for deep connection and understanding. Through respectful exploration, dedicated learning, sensitive photography, and supportive engagement, you help honor and preserve the cultural narratives that these sites safeguard. This profound respect and active preservation maintains the dignity and sanctity of the cultural heritage within our national parks, allowing them to be cherished and appreciated by all who come after.

6.6 Reporting Issues: How Visitors Can Help

The stewardship of our national parks is a collective endeavor that thrives on its visitors' active participation and vigilance. Each person who steps into these natural sanctuaries holds the potential to make a substantial impact, not just through their actions but also through their observations. The principle of "See Something, Say Something" plays a pivotal role in maintaining the safety and beauty of these parks. When visitors take it upon themselves to report instances of vandalism, wildlife harassment, or any unsafe or disrespectful behavior, they contribute directly to preserving the park's integrity. This proactive approach helps park authorities address issues promptly, ensuring that the parks remain pristine and welcoming.

Understanding how and where to report issues is crucial in making this system work effectively. Most parks provide several channels through which visitors can report problems or concerns. Visitor centers and ranger stations are the primary contact points where staff can take reports directly. For incidents away from these hubs, many parks offer emergency contact numbers that can be used to report issues directly to park management or law enforcement. In today's digital age, several parks provide online forms or email addresses for visitor reports. These multiple channels ensure that visitors can easily and immediately report any issues, no matter where in the park they are located.

Participation in volunteer programs offers another avenue through which visitors can contribute to the conservation and maintenance of park environments. These programs are designed to engage the public in direct conservation efforts, such as trail restoration, invasive species removal, and habitat rehabilitation. Volunteers provide valuable human resources and gain a deeper appreciation and understanding of the challenges involved in park maintenance. This hands-on involvement fosters a strong connection and responsibility towards the park, encouraging ongoing support and advocacy for conservation initiatives.

Providing constructive feedback and suggestions to park management is equally important. Visitor feedback is vital for improving the park experience and enhancing conservation efforts. Many parks conduct surveys or provide feedback forms that allow visitors to share their experiences and offer suggestions for improvements. This input can be invaluable in shaping park policies, visitor services, and educational programs, ensuring that they meet the needs and expectations of the public while promoting effective stewardship of natural resources.

Through these actions—reporting problems, participating in volunteer efforts, and providing feedback—visitors play an essential role in the stewardship of our national parks. This collaborative approach addresses immediate issues and fosters a proactive community dedicated to preserving the natural beauty and ecological integrity of these cherished landscapes.

As we close this chapter on safety, conservation, and etiquette, we reflect on each visitor's powerful role in protecting our national parks. Your vigilance, participation, and feedback are fundamental to preserving these natural treasures for future generations. Embracing these responsibilities enriches your experience and contributes to our national parks' sustainable management and conservation. As we transition to the next chapter, we carry forward the ethos of active participation and stewardship, ready to explore the myriad ways in which we can continue to enjoy and preserve the natural wonders of our world.

Chapter 7: Activities and Experiences

Figure 21 Easy Hiking Trail

Imagine the gentle rustle of leaves underfoot, the crisp air filling your lungs, and the unparalleled joy of reaching a viewpoint that stretches the horizons of both landscape and spirit. Hiking in America's national parks offers a spectrum of experiences that cater to every visitor, from the serene stroller to the adventurous trekker. This part of your journey through the parks is not just about physical paths but about discovering trails that challenge your body, elevate your spirit, and deepen your connection to the natural world.

7.1 Best National Park Hikes for Every Fitness Level

Easy Trails for Beginners

For those new to hiking or looking for a gentle day out with the family, national parks boast an array of scenic trails that promise beauty without strain. These paths are often well-maintained, flat, and feature plenty of rest spots with benches or informative placards. Consider the Trail of the Cedars in Glacier National Park, which offers an accessible boardwalk loop through an ancient forest, resonating with the sounds of nature and the lore of the land. Similarly, the Sunset Point Trail in Bryce Canyon provides a short, effortless walk with some of the most spectacular views of the park's famous spire-like rock formations. These trails not only make the great outdoors accessible to all ages and abilities but also serve as perfect introductions to the joys of hiking, ensuring everyone, regardless of fitness level, can experience the therapeutic benefits of spending time in nature.

Moderate Hikes

Moderate trails offer the perfect middle ground if you want to step up the challenge slightly. These paths might include elevation gain, uneven surfaces, or longer distances, but they reward hikers with more stunning vistas and quieter trails. In Yosemite National Park, the Mist Trail to Vernal Fall offers a moderately challenging hike that brings you up close to two of the park's majestic waterfalls. The trail can be steep and rocky, but the mist from the waterfalls and the panoramic views from the top provide a refreshing and exhilarating experience. Another gem is the Highline Trail in Glacier National Park, which starts from the Logan Pass and offers breathtaking views along a narrow path with steep drop-offs, thrilling for those with a head for heights. While requiring more stamina and preparation, these hikes are incredibly rewarding, offering unique experiences and views that will leave you intrigued and excited for more.

Strenuous Hikes

For the seasoned hiker seeking a test of endurance and a taste of adventure, the strenuous trails of America's national parks offer an enticing challenge. These trails demand a proficient level of fitness, appropriate gear, and a well-prepared mindset. The Half Dome hike in Yosemite, a demanding trek involving steep inclines, rock steps, and cable routes, is a bucket-list challenge that rewards the brave with unrivaled views from the summit. Another demanding hike is the Bright Angel Trail in Grand Canyon National Park, which takes you deep into the canyon and requires a full day (or more with a campground reservation). The physical demands of these trails are matched by their spectacular landscapes, providing a sense of achievement and awe that is hard to match.

Figure 22 Strenuous Hiking Trail

Accessibility on the Trails

Figure 23 ADA-accessible Trail

National parks are increasingly striving to make nature accessible to everyone, including visitors with mobility challenges. Many parks now feature ADA-accessible trails, offering firm, stable surfaces with minimal incline. They are often well-signed and provide regular resting points. The Pa'rus Trail in Zion National Park is one such trail, allowing wheelchair users and those with strollers to enjoy the park's scenic beauty alongside the Virgin River. Another notable mention is the Taggart Lake Trail in Grand Teton National Park, which offers an accessible route with compacted surfaces and gentle slopes, making the stunning views of the Teton Range available to all. These accessible trails underscore the parks' commitment to inclusivity, ensuring that the beauty of the wilderness is available to every visitor, regardless of physical ability.

Through these diverse hiking experiences, from leisurely walks to challenging treks, you traverse physical distances and journey through a landscape of growth, challenge, and deep connection with the natural world. Each trail offers a unique narrative, a story you become a part of, and memories that add to the rich tapestry of your life experiences. As you lace up your boots and set out on these trails, remember that every step takes you deeper into the heart of the park and closer to the wild heart of nature itself.

7.2 Capturing the Moment: Photography Tips for Amateurs

In the sprawling expanses of America's national parks, where the landscapes stretch boldly towards the horizon, and the light dances with the time of day, photography becomes more than just a hobby—it is a way to capture the essence of the earth's beauty and share it with the world. For those new to photography, understanding the basic principles can transform simple snapshots into stunning compositions that evoke the spirit of these majestic places.

The art of composition in photography is foundational, and it begins with learning how to frame your environment in ways that guide the viewer's eye to the heart of the scene. The rule of thirds is a classic technique where you imagine your frame divided into nine equal segments by two vertical and two horizontal lines. Placing points of interest at the intersections of these lines can create more tension, energy, and interest in your composition than simply centering on the subject. Moreover, incorporating leading lines—paths, rivers, or mountain ridges—that lead into the image can draw viewers deeper into the scene, making your photographs more engaging. Lighting also plays a critical role; the soft hues of golden hour, just after sunrise or before sunset, provide ideal lighting conditions that highlight textures and colors, lending a magical quality to your landscapes. Timing your photography sessions for these hours can significantly enhance the aesthetic appeal of your photos. Additionally, understanding the importance of timing in capturing the right moment, such as waiting for a gust of wind to animate a field of wildflowers or catching the fleeting light as it peeks through a dense forest, can add a dynamic element to your shots.

Investing in the right gear is crucial for amateur photographers eager to document their national park adventures. Starting with a reliable camera, whether a DSLR, a mirrorless model, or a high-quality compact, is fundamental. Each type offers different advantages, from DSLRs' versatility and high image quality to compact cameras' portability and simplicity. A tripod is another essential piece of equipment that provides stability for your camera, which is especially important in low light conditions or when capturing long exposures, such as flowing water or night skies. Additionally, a selection of lenses can enhance your ability to capture diverse landscapes. A wide-angle lens is perfect for expansive scenes, allowing you to include more of the environment, while a telephoto lens can bring distant features, like a mountain peak or wildlife, closer without disturbing the natural setting. Filters like polarizers can enhance colors and reduce reflections, making them valuable additions to your photography kit.

Ethical considerations in photography are paramount, especially in the sensitive ecosystems of national parks. Always maintain a respectful distance from wildlife, using your zoom lens to capture close-up images instead of approaching the animals. This ensures your safety and that of the wildlife and preserves the natural behavior of the creatures you photograph. Be mindful of the environment; stick to trails and public areas to avoid trampling native vegetation or causing erosion. When photographing landscapes, strive to leave no trace of your presence, ensuring that the beauty you capture remains undisturbed for others to enjoy. Moreover, consider the cultural significance of the sites you photograph, especially in areas that hold historical or spiritual importance to Indigenous communities. In such cases, seek to understand and respect any applicable photography restrictions.

Sharing your photographs on social media platforms offers a beautiful opportunity to convey the splendor of national parks to a broader audience, potentially inspiring others to appreciate and visit these natural treasures. When posting your images, consider the impact of geotagging specific locations. While sharing the beauty of lesser-known spots can lead to increased visitation, it can also result in environmental degradation if these areas are not equipped to handle more foot traffic. A responsible approach is to tag more general locations or the park rather than specific coordinates. Moreover, accompany your photos with captions that promote conservation messages or share interesting facts about the park's ecology, geology, or history. This educates your audience and fosters a deeper appreciation and respect for these natural environments. By embracing these practices, your photography can become a powerful tool for conservation, education, and inspiration, extending the impact of your national park experiences far beyond the visual images you capture.

7.3 The Park Ranger Experience: Programs and Tours

Engaging with park rangers during your visit to a national park can profoundly enhance your understanding and enjoyment of these protected areas' natural and historical contexts. With their wealth of knowledge and passion for environmental education and conservation, rangers serve as invaluable park guides, educators, and stewards. They offer a variety of programs and tours designed to deepen visitors' connections to the natural world through educational and interpretive experiences that cater to all ages and interests.

Ranger-led programs are a cornerstone of the educational offerings in national parks. These programs vary widely and may include guided hikes, wildlife-watching tours, and educational talks that explore the intricate ecosystems of the parks. For instance, a guided hike might focus on the geology of the Grand Canyon or the ancient life forms preserved in the fossil beds of Badlands National Park. During these walks, rangers share insights about the geological forces that shaped these landscapes and discuss how various life forms have adapted to their environments over millennia. Storytelling also plays a significant role in these programs, with rangers recounting the history of the parks, from the formation of their landscapes to the human histories that have crossed these terrains. These narratives inform and inspire a greater appreciation for the conservation efforts that preserve these spaces. Interactive elements such as asking questions or participating in hands-on activities can make these experiences more engaging, particularly for younger visitors, helping them to retain the information and feel a personal connection to the park.

Behind-the-scenes tours provide another layer of depth to the park experience, offering a glimpse into areas and operations that are typically inaccessible to the public. These unique tours might include visits to research facilities where scientists study flora and fauna or maintenance areas where conservation practices are implemented, such as controlled burns or reforestation projects. Such tours highlight the ongoing work necessary to maintain and protect these vast natural resources and underscore the challenges and complexities of park management. This insider view fosters a deeper understanding of the importance of resource management and the roles that various scientific and policy-driven initiatives play in sustaining the health of the parks' ecosystems.

For families visiting the parks, the Junior Ranger programs provide a structured and enjoyable way for children to learn about the natural environment and the responsibilities involved in its preservation. Through activities designed to be both fun and educational, children can earn Junior Ranger badges, which serve as symbols of their learning and their commitment to protecting natural resources. These programs often include completing educational worksheets, participating in clean-up activities, or attending ranger-led tours designed to teach young visitors about the importance of conservation and respectful recreation in natural settings.

The "Ask a Ranger" feature, available in many parks, allows visitors to interact directly with rangers via informal Q&A sessions. This resource is invaluable for visitors seeking specific information about the park, advice on must-see spots, or tips on safely exploring the park's more remote areas. Rangers can tailor their advice to the interests and capacities of each visitor, whether it is recommending a quiet spot for bird watching, the best time of day to photograph landscapes, or the most family-friendly hiking trails. This personalized interaction not only enhances visitor experience but also helps manage visitor impact on the most sensitive areas of the park.

Participating in these ranger-led programs and tours gives you a richer, more comprehensive understanding of the national parks. It contributes to the ongoing educational and conservation missions these programs support. Through these interactions, rangers share their knowledge and inspire visitors to become stewards of these natural treasures, ensuring their preservation for future generations. As you explore the diverse offerings of the Park Ranger Experience, you immerse yourself in a world where every trail tells a story, every creature has a role, and every visit leaves a lasting impact.

7.4 Nighttime in the Parks: From Campfires to Star Parties

When the sun dips below the horizon, and the first stars twinkle in the vast night sky, America's national parks transform into a new, mysterious world. This is when the air cools, the sounds of daytime creatures fade, and a different side of the park comes to life. Embracing the darkness of these protected lands offers unique opportunities for connection and discovery, from the communal warmth of campfire programs to the awe-inspiring spectacle of celestial events.

Campfire programs are a cherished tradition in many national parks, providing an enchanting way to wind down a day of exploration. Gathered around the crackling flames, you can enjoy various activities that bring the park's culture, history, and science to life. Park rangers or local experts often lead these sessions, sharing tales of the park's early inhabitants, recounting legendary exploration feats, or explaining the area's ecological importance. These stories, enhanced by the intimate, flickering light of the campfire, create a captivating atmosphere that enriches your understanding of the park. Sometimes, these gatherings are graced with cultural presentations, such as Native American storytelling or folk music performances, offering more profound insight into the region's cultural fabric. These programs educate and foster a sense of community among visitors, as families and strangers share in the timeless storytelling tradition under the open sky.

As night deepens, many parks host stargazing events that invite you to gaze upwards and marvel at the universe's wonders. These star parties are often held in collaboration with local astronomical societies, bringing telescopes and experienced astronomers to guide you through the night's features. Such events provide a spectacular visual journey through constellations, vivid planets, and meteor showers, all visible due to the minimal light pollution that national parks offer. The experience of seeing the Milky Way in its whole, luminous arc can be transformative, reminding you of the vastness of the universe and the beauty of our small place within it. Rangers often explain celestial phenomena and share stories of how ancient cultures interpreted the skies, adding cultural and scientific context layers that enhance the sense of wonder.

Figure 24 Stars over a campfire

For the adventurous, night hikes open a new perspective of the park's landscape, illuminated by stars and the moon's soft glow. Led by rangers, these guided walks take you into the heart of the park's nocturnal environment, where you can listen to the night sounds: the hoot of an owl, the rustle of small mammals in the underbrush, or the distant howl of coyotes. These hikes heighten your sensory experiences and teach you about the behaviors of nocturnal animals and their strategies to navigate the darker hours. The trails chosen for these hikes are usually well-suited for night-time walking, ensuring safety while offering a thrilling experience of the park after dark.

Capturing the magic of the night sky through photography is another enriching activity that many park visitors pursue. Nighttime photography in national parks, away from city lights, can yield stunning images of the sky's celestial bodies and the landscapes beneath them. Critical tips for successful night photography include using a tripod to stabilize your camera for long exposures, employing a remote shutter release to avoid camera shake, and setting your camera to a high ISO to capture the best light without too much noise. Focusing can be challenging in the dark, so setting your focus to infinity or using a bright star can help ensure sharp images. Additionally, experimenting with different shutter speeds can help you capture everything from detailed moonlit landscapes to sweeping star trails, depending on the artistic effect you are aiming for.

As you immerse yourself in these nighttime activities, the national parks reveal their hidden narratives and unseen spectacles, offering a profound connection to the natural world that resonates deep within. From the communal joy of campfires to the quiet solitude of a starlit hike, the night hours in these parks are a time for reflection, wonder, and deep, enduring memories.

7.5 The Solitude of Winter: Snowshoeing and Cross-Country Skiing

As the landscape dons its winter cloak, the national parks transform into serene, snowy wonderlands offering a quieter, more introspective adventure. Snowshoeing and cross-country skiing become delightful ways to traverse these frosty terrains, allowing you to glide across snow-blanketed trails while enveloped in the profound silence of winter. The experience is not just about physical activity; it is a chance to witness the parks draped in their winter finery, a stark contrast to the busy trails of summer.

Figure 25 A snowshoe trek through the park

Exploring the winter trails of parks like Yellowstone is a surreal experience where geothermal features steam against the backdrop of snow, and the crisp air is punctuated by the crunch of snow underfoot. Here, snowshoeing along the edges of the Upper Geyser Basin lets you experience the magic of Old Faithful and other geysers without the summer crowds, surrounded by snowfall's muffled stillness. For cross-country skiing, the terrains of Grand Teton National Park offer unparalleled opportunities. The groomed trails in the shadow of the

Teton Range, such as those in the Jenny Lake area, provide spectacular views and various distances and difficulties, catering to both novices and experienced skiers. With reliable snow conditions and scenic trails, these parks become havens for winter sports enthusiasts seeking beauty and solitude.

When preparing for snowshoeing or skiing in these frosty conditions, selecting the right gear is crucial to ensure comfort and safety. Your attire should focus on insulation and moisture management—layering is essential. Start with a moisture-wicking base layer to keep sweat away from your skin, add an insulating middle layer, such as fleece or down, and top it with a waterproof and windproof shell to guard against the elements. Footwear should also be waterproof and insulated, ideally with tall, gaiter-compatible cuffs to keep snow from entering your boots. For snowshoeing, choosing the right snowshoes is vital; consider the type of terrain and your weight (including your backpack) to determine the appropriate size and style. Similarly, selecting skis that suit the terrain and your skill level will enhance your experience for cross-country skiing. Poles with larger baskets are beneficial in deeper snow, helping to provide balance and propulsion.

Safety in winter park visits requires careful planning and awareness of cold and unpredictable weather challenges. Always check the weather forecast and trail conditions before heading out, and be prepared for rapid weather changes common in mountainous areas. Hypothermia is a risk if you get wet or cold, so bring extra clothing, an emergency shelter, and a means to make a fire. Navigation can be more challenging in the snow, as trails can be obscured and landmarks less visible. A GPS device, a detailed map, and a compass are essential tools. Additionally, understanding the signs of avalanche risk and knowing the terrain can be lifesaving, especially in mountain parks where slopes and accumulated snowpack can create hazardous conditions. Consider carrying avalanche safety equipment like a beacon, probe, and shovel if venturing into areas with avalanche potential. Lastly, always let someone know your plans and expected return time.

Winter also offers unique opportunities for wildlife watching as snow covers the landscape, making animals more visible against the white backdrop and their tracks easier to follow. This season brings a different rhythm to wildlife activity, with many animals displaying behaviors adapted to the cold. In parks like Rocky Mountain National Park, you might spot elk herds in the lower valleys or catch a glimpse of a bobcat as it navigates the snow. Smaller creatures like snowshoe hares, which turn white in the winter, become delightful subjects for observation and photography. When watching wildlife, keep a respectful distance to avoid causing animals stress, especially in winter when they are conserving energy to stay warm. Use binoculars or telephoto lenses to observe or photograph animals without disturbing them. Additionally, moving quietly and patiently can lead to more frequent and closer encounters as you blend more into the landscape, observing the natural behaviors of the park's winter residents.

As you embrace the tranquility and stark beauty of the parks in winter, snowshoeing and cross-country skiing offer exercise and a profound connection to nature. These activities allow you to explore areas that might be inaccessible at other times of the year and to experience the serene beauty of the parks under a blanket of snow. Whether following a well-trodden path or forging your own across a silent, snow-covered meadow, winter in the national parks is a season of discovery, reflection, and unparalleled beauty.

7.6 Water Activities: From Rafting to Fishing

The rhythmic dip of paddles in the still water, the exhilarating rush of river rapids, and the quiet patience of a fishing line cast into tranquil waters define the diverse water-based activities available in America's national parks. These activities offer unique perspectives of the park's landscapes and invite you to interact with the aquatic ecosystems in a physically engaging and environmentally respectful manner.

River rafting in national parks can range from gentle floats where the river's current lazily guides your raft to adrenaline-pumping white-water experiences that challenge even seasoned rafters. Parks such as the Grand Canyon National Park offer iconic rafting experiences that combine breathtaking canyon views with the thrill of navigating the Colorado River's rapids. Rafting here can vary from a few hours to multi-week adventures, providing opportunities to camp along riverbanks and explore side canyons. Another notable destination for rafting enthusiasts is the New River Gorge National Park, renowned for its powerful rapids and stunning Appalachian scenery. For beginners eager to experience river rafting, many parks provide guided tours where experienced guides manage the navigation, allowing you to fully immerse yourself in the experience and the natural beauty surrounding you. These guided adventures also often include educational components, where you learn about the river's ecology and the geological forces that shaped its course.

Figure 26 Fishing in a National Park

Fishing in national parks offers a serene escape and a chance to engage with the park's wildlife. However, it is crucial to understand and follow the specific fishing regulations, which vary from park to park. These regulations are crafted to balance recreational opportunities with conservation efforts, ensuring sustainable fish populations. For instance, Yellowstone National Park requires a permit for fishing, which can be obtained at visitor centers or nearby towns. The park has specific rules about which fish may be kept or need to be released and restrictions on the types of bait and tackle permitted to protect native fish species and prevent the introduction of pathogens. Before heading out, familiarize yourself with these regulations, available on the park's website or at park ranger stations, to ensure your fishing activities support the health of the park's aquatic ecosystems.

Kayaking and canoeing in national parks allow you to explore waterways often inaccessible by foot or vehicle, offering quiet solitude and intimacy with nature. Quiet paddles through the mangrove swamps of Everglades National Park or gliding across the mirrored surface of Grand Teton National Park's Jenny Lake can be peaceful yet profound experiences. These activities require minimal gear, and many parks offer rental services at major lakes or rivers, making getting on the water easy. Additionally, kayaking and canoeing have a minimal environmental impact, making them excellent ways to explore sensitive habitats without disturbing wildlife. As you paddle, observe the aquatic plants, watch birds, and enjoy the gentle splash of water against your boat, creating a rhythm that enhances your connection to the natural world.

Adhering to Leave No Trace principles during water-based activities is essential to protect the aquatic environments of these parks. Practice carrying in all your needed supplies and carrying out all trash, including bait and food scraps, which can disrupt local wildlife habits and water quality. Be mindful of where you launch and land your kayak or canoe, using designated areas to avoid damaging sensitive shoreline vegetation. Additionally, cleaning your watercraft before entering and after leaving park waters can prevent the spread of invasive species, which can devastate local ecosystems. These practices ensure that the park's waters remain pristine for fellow visitors and the wildlife that call these waters home.

Engaging in water-based activities in national parks allows you to experience the parks' landscapes from a unique and enriching perspective. Whether navigating the rapids of a mighty river, casting a line into a crystal-clear lake, or paddling quietly along a peaceful stream, these activities offer more than just physical benefits; they deepen your ecological awareness and foster a stronger connection to the natural world. As you move through these waterways, you become a witness to the subtle rhythms of aquatic life, the changing lights on the water's surface, and the grandeur of the landscapes that frame these aquatic adventures.

As we close this chapter on the diverse water-based activities available in America's national parks, we reflect on the profound connections these experiences foster with the natural world. From the adrenaline of river rafting to the tranquility of fishing, each activity offers a pathway to appreciate and engage with the park's aquatic environments. By participating responsibly and with environmental consciousness, you contribute to preserving these valuable ecosystems. Looking ahead, the journey through America's national parks unfolds with more adventures and opportunities to connect with nature in profound and transformative ways.

Chapter 8: Beyond the Beaten Path

8.1 North Cascades National Park: America's Best-Kept Secret

Imagine threading through a landscape where the whispers of the wind carry stories of hidden realms and rugged beauty untouched by the clamor of crowded tourist spots. This is the essence of North Cascades National Park, a treasure trove of natural splendor that remains one of the least explored parks in the United States. Here, the call of the wild is a metaphor and a palpable presence amid jagged peaks, deep valleys, and cascading waterfalls, inviting you, the intrepid explorer, to uncover its secrets.

Hidden Hikes and Views

One of the park's most compelling draws is its network of lesser-known trails, each offering a unique vantage point and solitude that is becoming increasingly rare in more frequented parks. For instance, the Hidden Lake Lookout trail provides a rigorous but rewarding hike leading to an old fire lookout, from where you can gaze out over a panorama of serrated peaks and sprawling wilderness. Another hidden gem is the Thunder Creek Trail, which meanders through ancient forests alongside the melodious Thunder Creek, offering glimpses of distant glaciers. These paths are not just routes through the park but journeys into its very heart, revealing the grandeur and the quiet majesty of the North Cascades at every turn.

Local Wildlife

The park is a sanctuary for diverse wildlife, each species adapted to the rugged life of the high mountains. From the elusive gray wolf to the majestic mountain goat and the cunning lynx, the park offers a chance to encounter these creatures in their natural habitats. Observing these animals, however, requires patience and respect for their space and needs. Best practices for wildlife watching include keeping a safe distance, using binoculars for up-close views, and avoiding interference with their natural activities. Early mornings or late evenings are typically the best times to watch wildlife, as these are the hours when many animals are most active.

Seasonal Highlights

Each season paints the park in new colors and brings different experiences. Spring arrives late but transforms the landscape rapidly, with wildflowers such as lupines and Indian paintbrushes bursting into vibrant life against the melting snow. Summer offers the most access to high trails and the best weather for camping under the star-lit sky, while autumn cloaks the park in fiery hues, and the air is crisp with the promise of coming snow. Winter turns the park into a quiet, snowy wonderland, ideal for snowshoeing and witnessing the serene beauty of the snow-capped peaks. Each season offers unique sights and activities, making the park a year-round destination for those seeking solitude and natural beauty.

Conservation Efforts

Visiting North Cascades is a privilege, and with it comes the responsibility to help preserve this wild landscape. Efforts to protect the park can be as simple as adhering to trails to prevent soil erosion, carrying out all trash to keep the park clean, and using bear-proof containers to protect wildlife. Participating in volunteer programs such as trail maintenance or educational outreach can also make a significant positive impact. These actions help ensure the park's ecosystem thrives and remains a sanctuary for wildlife and human visitors.

In this hidden corner of the world, you find a profound connection to nature that is both humbling and exhilarating. North Cascades National Park offers more than just a retreat from the modern world; it provides a chance to engage deeply with the wild, learn from it, and be part of its ongoing story of conservation and discovery. Here, in the silence of the ancient forests and the vastness of the open skies, you are invited to rediscover the wonder of the wild, find peace in its untouched beauty, and carry forward the call of conservation that safeguards these treasures for future generations.

8.2 The Quiet Side of Grand Canyon: North Rim Adventures

Venturing into the Grand Canyon, one of the world's true natural wonders presents a tale of two rims: the bustling South Rim, known for its accessibility and panoramic viewpoints, and the secluded North Rim, which offers a peaceful retreat into nature's embrace. While the South Rim attracts most of the park's visitors, the North Rim provides a sanctuary for those seeking solitude and a deeper connection with the rugged landscape. The North Rim, perched at a higher elevation, boasts fewer amenities but offers a more intimate and contemplative canyon experience. This part of the park, open seasonally due to heavy winter snows, entices with its raw beauty and quieter trails, where the sounds of nature prevail over the crowds.

The trails on the North Rim do not merely serve as paths—they are passageways into the heart of the canyon's majesty. One such trail, the North Kaibab Trail, offers an immersive experience as it descends into the canyon, revealing layers of geological history with each step. The Cape Royal Trail provides a less strenuous, equally rewarding journey for those not venturing deep into the canyon. This trail leads to an expansive viewpoint where the canyon's grandeur unfolds in a breathtaking panorama, encompassing the Colorado River and the ragged peaks beyond. Each trail presents its narrative, inviting you to partake in the story of ancient stones and timeless vistas.

Choosing the best time to visit the North Rim is crucial for those who prefer tranquility over hustle. The rim is accessible from mid-May to mid-October, with the peak visitor months being June through August. To savor the peace, consider visiting in late May or early October when the days are still warm and the nights hint at the crisp autumn air. During these times, the changing colors of the expansive forest surrounding the rim add a brushstroke of vibrant hues to the already stunning scenery, enhancing the visual feast. Moreover, these shoulder seasons allow for a more leisurely exploration of the rim, where one can linger at viewpoints or rest on quiet trails with only the whisper of the wind for company.

Figure 27 Grand Canyon

The North Rim also serves as a haven for various flora and fauna that thrive in its higher elevation and cooler temperatures. The mixed conifer forests, a rarity in the canyon's arid regions, offer a green oasis that contrasts sharply with the stark rock faces. These forests are home to species unique to the area, such as the Kaibab squirrel, with distinctive tufted ears and bushy tails. Bird enthusiasts might glimpse the rare California condor, an impressive sight as it soars against the blue sky, riding the thermals above the canyon. These species' presence highlights the rim's ecological diversity and underscores the importance of preserving such habitats. As you walk the trails or scan the skies, remember that these creatures are not merely passing through—they are an integral part of the canyon's ecosystem, each maintaining the delicate balance of this rugged landscape.

8.3 Exploring the Lesser-Known Islands of Channel Islands National Park

Off the coast of Southern California, where the Pacific's deep blue meets the rugged cliffs, lies the Channel Islands National Park. This park, often overlooked in favor of its more accessible mainland counterparts, offers a serene escape into a world where nature thrives undisturbed by urban sprawl. The park comprises five remarkable islands, each boasting its unique ecosystem and adventures that beckon the ardent explorer. Island hopping here is not just a leisure activity but an exploration into diverse ecological havens, each island a different chapter of a vast, unfolding natural story. Planning a visit to these less trodden islands—like San Miguel with its vast seal rookeries or Santa Rosa, home to rare Torrey pines—requires a keen sense of adventure and a readiness to embrace nature's raw, elemental beauty.

Each island's distinct ecosystem offers a vibrant tableau of biodiversity. Santa Cruz Island, the largest in the archipelago, presents a varied landscape of high peaks and deep canyons with lush oak woodlands and the endemic Santa Cruz Island fox. This small, curious creature has adapted splendidly to its isolated environment. Meanwhile, though stark and rugged, the tiny Anacapa Island bursts into color with coreopsis blooms in the spring, creating a striking contrast against the backdrop of sheer cliffs and the ocean beyond. These islands serve as a refuge for these unique species and as natural laboratories, offering invaluable insights into ecological balance and evolutionary processes. The isolation of these islands has led to high rates of endemism, which means many species found here are native only to these islands and nowhere else on Earth, making the park a critical preserve for biological diversity.

Adventure on these islands is as varied as the ecosystems themselves. Kayaking along the kelp-rich waters of Scorpion Anchorage offers a tranquil yet invigorating experience, with opportunities to glide alongside playful sea lions and curious dolphins. For those who favor the underwater realms, snorkeling in the kelp forests around the islands reveals a bustling community of marine life—bright orange Garibaldi fish, spiny lobsters, and an array of starfish decorate these underwater forests. Hiking trails wind through each island, offering everything from leisurely walks to challenging hikes. On Santa Rosa Island, for instance, a hike to Black Mountain provides breathtaking views of the Channel Islands, while a more leisurely path might lead you through historic ranches and the island's stunning beaches.

Conservation is a crucial theme in the stewardship of Channel Islands National Park. The delicate balance of these ecosystems makes them particularly susceptible to external pressures, including invasive species, which visitors can introduce inadvertently. Efforts to preserve the native flora and fauna here are robust and continuous. Programs aimed at removing non-native species and restoring habitats are critical to maintaining the ecological integrity of the islands. Visitors play a crucial role in these conservation efforts; by respecting guidelines, such as staying on marked trails and ensuring no biological material or non-native species are brought onto the islands, they help protect these fragile environments. Furthermore, engaging with the park's educational programs helps spread awareness about the importance of conservation and the challenges these unique ecosystems face. These programs often include guided tours that elucidate the islands' natural and cultural histories, fostering a deeper appreciation and a strong conservation ethic among visitors.

The Channel Islands offer a rare opportunity to experience untouched wilderness, where the interplay of sea, land, and life creates a dynamic environment that is as educational as it is breathtaking. Here, the rhythm of the ocean dictates life, both in the water and on the rugged shores. For those willing to journey, the Channel Islands reveal the beauty and complexity of nature's undisturbed state, a precious reminder of the wild that once was and what we must strive to protect. Whether tracing the graceful arc of a kayaking paddle through the water, marveling at the agile leap of a fox, or simply absorbing the serene beauty of an untouched landscape, the islands offer endless moments of connection to the natural world, each visit contributing to the ongoing story of preservation and discovery in this exceptional national park.

8.4 Biking Through Big South Fork National River and Recreation Area

Nestled on the Cumberland Plateau, the Big South Fork National River and Recreation Area offers a refreshing escape with its rich tapestry of deep gorges, towering sandstone bluffs, and lush wooded valleys. For biking enthusiasts, this park serves as a prime destination, featuring a variety of trails that cater to mountain bikers seeking thrilling rides and those preferring scenic, leisurely cycles. The park's well-maintained trails, such as the Collier Ridge Bike Loop and the West Bandy Trail, offer diverse biking experiences that allow you to immerse yourself deeply in the natural beauty and serenity of the area. The Collier Ridge loop, for example, challenges riders with its rises and dips while providing occasional clearings that offer stunning views of the river's gorge. For a less strenuous experience, the gentler John Muir Trail follows historic paths that trace the river's edge, offering a peaceful ride with frequent views of the flowing waters and overhanging cliffs.

When preparing for a cycling adventure in Big South Fork, it is crucial to consider the safety and the specific demands of biking in remote areas. Safety starts with the right gear: a well-fitted helmet, gloves for grip and protection, and appropriate eyewear to shield against sunlight and flying debris. Considering the park's varied terrain, a mountain bike with durable tires and reliable suspension is advisable to navigate rocky paths and sudden inclines comfortably. It is also wise to carry a basic repair kit, including a spare tube, a multi-tool, and a hand pump, ensuring minor breakdowns do not end your ride prematurely. Since mobile reception can be spotty in remote areas, prepare a route map and share your travel plan with someone before you depart. Always check weather forecasts in advance to avoid being caught unprepared by sudden weather changes typical of the Plateau's climate.

The historical and cultural sites accessible via bike within Big South Fork notably enrich the cycling experience, connecting you with the area's rich heritage. Biking the Oscar Blevins Farm Loop, you encounter well-preserved homesteads that offer a glimpse into the life of early settlers and the challenges they faced in these rugged landscapes. Interpretive signs along the way narrate stories of the communities that once thrived here, providing a compelling historical context to the ride. Additionally, the park's former coal mining sites can be accessed on specific trails where abandoned mines and railroads tell a darker yet vital story of the region's industrial past. These sites serve as physical remnants of history and solemn reminders of the human will to adapt and survive in the harshest of environments.

The wildlife and scenery you encounter while biking in Big South Fork significantly enhance the journey, transforming each pedal stroke into an opportunity for discovery and connection with nature. The park's diverse ecosystems support an array of wildlife: white-tailed deer, wild turkeys, and occasionally, the elusive bobcat can be spotted along quieter trails, especially during the early hours of the morning or late afternoon. Birdwatchers might delight in catching sight of warblers, owls, and woodpeckers that inhabit the dense canopies. The flora is equally captivating, with each season painting the landscape in different hues. Spring rides are adorned with wildflowers like mountain laurel and flame azalea, while autumn transforms the trails into a vibrant mosaic of gold, orange, and red leaves. Riding through such dynamic scenery, you are reminded of nature's fleeting yet recurrent beauty, cycling not just through space, but through the ongoing cycle of life that defines this mesmerizing landscape.

8.5 Bird Watching in Congaree National Park: A Hidden Gem

Nestled in the heart of South Carolina, Congaree National Park offers a sanctuary for its majestic old-growth bottomland hardwood forest and a remarkable diversity of bird species. This park, often less traversed by the casual visitor, unfolds as a paradise for bird watchers, where the dense canopy and fertile floodplains support a vibrant avian community. From the Barred Owl's haunting call to the Prothonotary Warbler's vibrant flash, the park's avian inhabitants add a dynamic layer of life to the serene landscape.

Congaree's bird population is as diverse as the ecosystem, providing a home to permanent residents and migratory visitors. The park's extensive canopy, one of the tallest deciduous forest canopies in the world, offers an ideal habitat for species like the Wood Thrush and the Red-shouldered Hawk. Meanwhile, the lower strata and forest floor provide foraging grounds for the Wild Turkey and various species of woodpeckers, including the Pileated Woodpecker, whose distinctive drumming reverberates through the woods. The park's waterways and swamps attract wading birds like the Great Blue Heron and the elusive American Bittern. During migration periods, the variety expands dramatically, with species like the Black-throated Green Warbler and the American Redstart stopping in the park to refuel during their long journeys.

Timing your visit to maximize bird-watching success involves a strategic understanding of avian life cycles and migrations. The best times to visit Congaree for bird watching are during the spring and fall migrations, when the variety of species peaks dramatically. Early morning is typically the prime time for bird activity, as many species are most vocal and active during the first hours after dawn. This period increases your chances of seeing birds and experiencing their melodic calls, an auditory landscape that enhances the park's tranquility. Additionally, visiting after rain can prove fruitful, as many birds will emerge to feed, taking advantage of the moist conditions that make insects and other food sources more accessible.

For those new to bird watching or even seasoned birders looking to refine their skills, Congaree National Park offers an enriching environment to learn and practice. One essential technique is learning to bird by ear, which involves identifying birds through their calls and songs—a helpful method in a park where dense foliage often keeps birds hidden. Start with familiarizing yourself with the calls of common species, which can be done through various birding apps or field guides that provide audio samples. Patience and stillness are also vital; sitting quietly in one spot often proves more effective than covering a lot of ground. Bring binoculars with sound light transmission to help spot birds in the shadowy undergrowth and a field guide to assist in identification. For those interested in documenting their sightings, a notebook or a birding app to record the details of each encounter can enhance the experience and provide valuable data for conservation efforts.

Conservation awareness is integral to bird watching, especially in a biodiverse sanctuary like Congaree National Park. The park is a critical habitat for many bird species, some sensitive to environmental changes and human disturbances. Bird watchers can contribute to conservation efforts by adhering to park guidelines, such as staying on boardwalks and designated trails to avoid disturbing nesting sites and sensitive ecological areas. Participating in citizen science projects, such as bird counts or breeding surveys, can provide crucial data that helps park management and conservation organizations monitor and protect bird populations. Moreover, educating oneself about the ecological roles of different bird species can deepen an understanding of the ecosystem, fostering a greater appreciation and a more profound commitment to preserving these natural environments.

In Congaree National Park, each visit unfolds as a unique narrative written in the flight patterns of birds against the backdrop of towering trees and reflective waters. Here, the quiet observer witnesses the beauty of avian life and participates in a larger story of ecological awareness and conservation. With its rich bird diversity and pristine landscapes, the park offers more than just a bird-watching experience—it provides an invitation to connect with the natural world, learn from its rhythms, and contribute to its preservation. In this way, bird watching in Congaree becomes a pathway to deeper environmental connection and stewardship, a journey that is as rewarding to the spirit as it benefits the earth.

8.6 Backpacking in Isle Royale National Park: Tips for a Remote Adventure

Isle Royale National Park, set in the vast waters of Lake Superior, offers one of the most unique backpacking experiences in the United States. This remote island, accessible only by boat or seaplane, promises solitude and intimate communion with nature. It is a premier destination for those seeking a more profound wilderness experience. Planning a trip to this isolated paradise requires careful consideration and preparation to ensure safety and enjoyment.

When planning your backpacking trip to Isle Royale, the first step is to determine the duration and timing of your visit. The park is open from late April through October, and the best times to visit are late spring and early fall when the mosquitoes are less prevalent and the weather is mild. Due to its remote location, all visitors must arrive by boat or seaplane, so booking your transport well in advance is crucial. Once on the island, you must register for a backcountry permit at the visitor center, a necessary step to help manage the park's wilderness character. It is also wise to plan your route and overnight camping sites using the park's detailed maps. Given the limited resources on the island, carrying a well-stocked supply kit—including food, water purification systems, and a first-aid kit—is essential. Packing lightly but efficiently is crucial, as you must carry all your supplies throughout your hike.

Several backpacking routes offer a range of experiences, from easy hikes along the shoreline to challenging treks across the rugged island interior. For beginners, a trek from Rock Harbor to Daisy Farm offers well-maintained trails and stunning lakeside views, providing a gentle introduction to the island's landscapes. More experienced hikers might opt for the Greenstone Ridge Trail, which runs the island's length and offers panoramic views from the island's highest ridges. This route also allows for multiple side trips to smaller lakes and less-visited spots, offering a deeper exploration of the island's varied terrains. Each trail provides unique encounters with the island's raw beauty, from dense forests and serene lakes to rocky shores and high ridges, making each step a discovery.

Practicing the Leave No Trace principle is vital in preserving the pristine environment of Isle Royale. Given its designation as a wilderness area and a national park, the impact of human activity must be minimized. This includes setting up camps only in designated areas, using portable stoves instead of making campfires, and ensuring all waste is packed out or disposed of in designated areas. Sticking to established trails helps prevent soil erosion and protects plant life. Additionally, using biodegradable soaps and avoiding introducing non-native species are critical practices for maintaining the island's ecological balance.

Encounters with wildlife, including moose and wolves, are among the highlights of a visit to Isle Royale. Yet, they require careful management to ensure the safety of both the animals and visitors. Observing wildlife from a distance is crucial; approaching or feeding animals is dangerous and disrupts their natural behaviors. Noise should be kept to a minimum to avoid disturbing the wildlife, especially during the early morning and late evening when many species are most active. If you encounter a moose or wolf on the trail, it is vital to give them a wide berth, slowly backing away while avoiding sudden movements. Understanding and respecting these animals' behaviors ensures your safety and protects the integrity of their natural habitats.

In Isle Royale, each step into its wilderness is a step into a broader narrative of conservation, adventure, and the profound tranquility of untouched nature. This park is not just a destination; it is an invitation to embrace the natural world's rhythms, find solitude in its expansive landscapes, and contribute to preserving one of America's most isolated national parks. As you pack your backpack and set off across the island, you carry not just your supplies but a responsibility to tread lightly and a privilege to witness one of the most secluded natural environments in the United States.

As we close this chapter on Isle Royale National Park, we reflect on the crucial balance between exploring and preserving these remote wilderness areas. The insights gained here extend beyond just practical tips for backpacking; they are a call to integrate deep respect for nature into our adventures. This narrative of mindful exploration continues in the next chapter, where we uncover more hidden gems within America's vast network of national parks, each offering unique challenges and rewards.

Conclusion

As we draw the curtains on this journey through America's national parks, let us take a moment to reflect on the vast tapestry of landscapes we have traversed together. Each park has unfolded its unique story, from the awe-inspiring peaks of the Rocky Mountains to the serene expanses of the Mojave Desert, from the verdant forests of the Smoky Mountains to the rugged coastlines of Acadia. These are spaces of natural beauty and sanctuaries where the spirit of the wild invites us to step back from our daily grind and breathe in the essence of the earth itself.

The core mission of this book has been to serve not just as a guide but as an inspiration—a beacon to light your way as you navigate the grandeur of our national heritage. It has been crafted to enrich your journeys, equip you with the knowledge to tread softly and respectfully on these sacred grounds, and ensure that each visit is as rewarding as it is enlightening.

Among the key takeaways, remember the importance of preparation, the joy of discovery, and the duty of conservation. These parks are landscapes and legacies entrusted to us to protect and pass on to future generations. As we have explored these natural wonders together, we have seen how each park contributes to the mosaic of America's natural and cultural heritage and how crucial our role is in sustaining its beauty and vitality.

This brings us to a call to action that extends beyond mere visits. I urge you to become a steward of these treasures. Engage in community efforts to preserve these lands, advocate for their protection, and educate others about the importance of these natural resources. Our national parks do not just need visitors; they need champions.

The transformative power of nature is undeniable. In the quiet majesty of these parks, many find a rejuvenation of the soul and a fresh perspective on life. I encourage you to seek these experiences, to allow the silence of the forests, the majesty of the mountains, and the expanse of the deserts to seep into you and fill you with a renewed sense of wonder and peace.

On a personal note, each visit to these parks has deepened my connection not only to the natural world but also to the core of my being. These journeys have been a source of inspiration and contemplation, reminding me of the intricate connections that sustain us all. I hope to share this profound impact with you, inviting you to embark on your own journeys of discovery and exploration.

Thank you for joining me on this adventure through the pages of this book. May it be a companion on many fulfilling travels and a reminder of the endless wonders that await in our national parks. Continue to explore, learn, and conserve. The trails are many, the experiences vast, and the memories waiting to be made are countless. Let us step forward with a commitment to preserve these wonders for future generations.

List of America's National Parks

Acadia - Maine
American Samoa - American Samoa
Arches - Utah
Badlands - South Dakota
Big Bend - Texas
Biscayne - Florida
Black Canyon of the Gunnison - Colorado
Bryce Canyon - Utah
Canyonlands - Utah
Capitol Reef - Utah
Carlsbad Caverns - New Mexico
Channel Islands - California
Congaree - South Carolina
Crater Lake - Oregon
Cuyahoga Valley - Ohio
Death Valley - California, Nevada
Denali - Alaska
Dry Tortugas - Florida
Everglades - Florida
Gates of the Arctic - Alaska
Gateway Arch - Missouri
Glacier - Montana
Glacier Bay - Alaska
Grand Canyon - Arizona
Grand Teton - Wyoming
Great Basin - Nevada
Great Sand Dunes - Colorado
Great Smoky Mountains - North Carolina, Tennessee
Guadalupe Mountains - Texas
Haleakalā - Hawaii
Hawaii Volcanoes - Hawaii
Hot Springs - Arkansas
Indiana Dunes - Indiana
Isle Royale - Michigan
Joshua Tree - California
Katmai - Alaska
Kenai Fjords - Alaska

Kings Canyon - California
Kobuk Valley - Alaska
Lake Clark - Alaska
Lassen Volcanic - California
Mammoth Cave - Kentucky
Mesa Verde - Colorado
Mount Rainier - Washington
North Cascades - Washington
Olympic - Washington
Petrified Forest - Arizona
Pinnacles - California
Redwood - California
Rocky Mountain - Colorado
Saguaro - Arizona
Sequoia - California
Shenandoah - Virginia
Theodore Roosevelt - North Dakota
Virgin Islands - U.S. Virgin Islands
Voyageurs - Minnesota
White Sands - New Mexico
Wind Cave - South Dakota
Wrangell-St. Elias - Alaska
Yellowstone - Wyoming, Montana, Idaho
Yosemite - California
Zion - Utah

References

1. 10 things to know about a national park pass. (n.d.). *Reader's Digest*. Retrieved from https://www.rd.com/article/national-park-pass/
2. 10 tips to prevent wildfires | U.S. Department of the Interior. (n.d.). *U.S. Department of the Interior*. Retrieved from https://www.doi.gov/blog/10-tips-prevent-wildfires
3. 20 epic day hikes in the national parks (USA). (n.d.). *Earth Trekkers*. Retrieved from https://www.earthtrekkers.com/best-day-hikes-in-the-national-parks/
4. 7 ways to safely watch wildlife - National Park Service. (n.d.). *National Park Service*. Retrieved from https://www.nps.gov/subjects/watchingwildlife/7ways.htm
5. Accessible nature: A trail guide for disabled hikers. (2023, June 19). *The New York Times*. Retrieved from https://www.nytimes.com/2023/06/19/travel/disabled-hikers-park-guide.html
6. Avoiding crowds in national parks — even at the busiest times. (n.d.). *Wendy Perrin*. Retrieved from https://www.wendyperrin.com/avoiding-crowds-national-parks-even-busiest-times/
7. Backpacking & camping - Isle Royale National Park (U.S. National Park Service). (n.d.). *National Park Service*. Retrieved from https://www.nps.gov/isro/planyourvisit/camping.htm
8. Beginner's photography guide. (n.d.). *National Park Service*. Retrieved from https://www.nps.gov/articles/photographyguide.htm
9. Best Yosemite hikes away from the crowds. (n.d.). *OARS*. Retrieved from https://www.oars.com/blog/best-yosemite-hikes-away-crowds/
10. Camping Hiking. (n.d.). *How to stay warm and dry during a camping trip in cold or wet weather*. Retrieved June 7, 2024, from https://campinghiking.net/camping/how-to-stay-warm-and-dry-during-a-camping-trip-in-cold-or-wet-weather/
11. Canoe and kayak trails - Everglades National Park (U.S. National Park Service). (n.d.). *National Park Service*. Retrieved from https://www.nps.gov/ever/planyourvisit/canoe-and-kayak-trails.htm
12. Coral reef protection - Friends of Virgin Islands National Park. (n.d.). *Friends of Virgin Islands National Park*. Retrieved from https://friendsvinp.org/coral-reef-protection/

13. Geologic formations - Petrified Forest National Park (U.S. National Park Service). (n.d.). National Park Service. Retrieved from https://www.nps.gov/pefo/learn/nature/geologicformations.htm
14. Global code of ethics for tourism. (n.d.). United Nations World Tourism Organization. Retrieved from http://www.unwto.org/global-code-of-ethics-for-tourism
15. Grand Canyon North Rim vs South Rim: 10 key differences. (n.d.). Travel Awaits. Retrieved from https://www.travelawaits.com/2563372/grand-canyon-north-rim-vs-south-rim/
16. Halema'uma'u Crater (n.d.) Retrieved from https://volcanoes.usgs.gov/observatories/hvo
17. Hidden Lake Lookout — Washington Trails Association. (n.d.). Washington Trails Association. Retrieved from https://www.wta.org/go-hiking/hikes/hidden-lake-lookout
18. Leave no trace seven principles - National Park Service. (n.d.). National Park Service. Retrieved from https://www.nps.gov/articles/leave-no-trace-seven-principles.htm
19. Night skies and stargazing - Big Bend National Park (U.S. National Park Service). (n.d.). National Park Service. Retrieved from https://www.nps.gov/bibe/planyourvisit/stargazing.htm
20. Night skies: Beyond the Badlands (U.S. National Park Service). (n.d.). National Park Service. Retrieved from https://www.nps.gov/articles/000/night-skies-badl.htm
21. Photography - Arches National Park (U.S. National Park Service). (n.d.). National Park Service. Retrieved from https://www.nps.gov/arch/planyourvisit/photography.htm
22. Preparing for high elevation in Rocky Mountain National Park. (n.d.). Rocky Mountain National Park. Retrieved from https://www.rockymountainnationalpark.com/gallery/elevation/
23. Ranger programs in Yellowstone National Park. (n.d.). Frommer's. Retrieved from https://www.frommers.com/destinations/yellowstone-national-park/ranger-programs
24. Safety - Grand Teton National Park (U.S. National Park Service). (n.d.). National Park Service. Retrieved from https://www.nps.gov/grte/planyourvisit/safety.htm
25. Safety - Hawai'i Volcanoes National Park (U.S. National Park Service). (n.d.). National Park Service. Retrieved from https://www.nps.gov/havo/planyourvisit/safety.htm

26. Santa Cruz Island in California. (n.d.). The Nature Conservancy. Retrieved from https://www.nature.org/en-us/get-involved/how-to-help/places-we-protect/santa-cruz-island-california/
27. Shh! Secret places in Yellowstone for an intimate experience. (n.d.). Xanterra. Retrieved from https://www.xanterra.com/stories/shh-secret-places-in-yellowstone-for-an-intimate-experience/
28. Stargazing - Joshua Tree National Park (U.S. National Park Service). (n.d.). National Park Service. Retrieved from https://www.nps.gov/jotr/planyourvisit/stargazing.htm
29. The 7 principles - Leave No Trace Center for Outdoor Ethics. (n.d.). Leave No Trace Center for Outdoor Ethics. Retrieved from https://lnt.org/why/7-principles/
30. Tidepool activities on the coast of Olympic National Park (U.S. National Park Service). (n.d.). National Park Service. Retrieved from https://www.nps.gov/olym/planyourvisit/tidepool-activities.htm
31. Wildflowers - Great Smoky Mountains National Park (U.S. National Park Service). (n.d.). National Park Service. Retrieved from https://www.nps.gov/grsm/learn/nature/wildflowers.htm
32. Wildlife viewing - Theodore Roosevelt National Park (U.S. National Park Service). (n.d.). National Park Service. Retrieved from https://www.nps.gov/thro/planyourvisit/wildlife-viewing.htm
33. Your ultimate national park packing list for 2024. (n.d.). Organized Adventurer. Retrieved from https://organizedadventurer.com/national-parks-packing-list/

Keeping the Game Alive

Now that you have everything you need to explore our national parks, it is time to pass on your new knowledge and show other readers where they can find the same help.

Leaving your honest opinion of this book on Amazon will show other explorers where they can find the information they are looking for and share their passion for our national parks.

I appreciate your help. Our National Parks are kept alive when we pass on our knowledge – and you are helping me to do just that.

Simply scan the QR code below to leave your review:

Made in the USA
Columbia, SC
27 July 2024

a44da001-5465-4e82-98a0-ecd5887bb5b3R01